HOW TO TALK ABOUT GUNS WITH ANYONE

HOW TO TALK ABOUT GUNS WITH ANYONE

KATHERINE SCHWEIT

To learn more or to contact the author, please visit katherineschweit.com.

Paperback ISBN: 978-1-947635-58-6
Ebook ISBN: 978-1-947635-59-3

To those long dedicated to battling gun violence
and those now willing to step into the fray.

CONTENTS

Foreword

Guns. They have been a part of my life since I was a little boy in the backyard, playing the role of the sheriff with my silver six gun and the brown holster that came in a plastic package from the five and dime.

As a young crime reporter in New York City, I saw the real world of gun violence while covering stories in a city where 85 percent of the murders were committed with firearms. Later, working in the LAPD, the NYPD, and the FBI, I carried guns. These weapons came with a good deal of training and a great deal of responsibility. These were the functional black pistols specifically built for self-defense. But I have known other guns in different ways; the beautifully crafted walnut stock and metal barrel of my over-and-under shotgun I have used to shoot skeet and trap with my friends for sport.

I have known cops and criminals, soldiers, and sportsmen, albeit in distinctly different ways. My heroes carried guns and so did my enemies. This was reinforced for me in those places where cops, agents and reporters end up, at scenes of murders, multiple mass shootings, wars, emergency rooms, and too many police funerals. We all see the impact of guns in our world. It plays as part of the surround sound of cable news and social media and follows us through our days.

All these experiences have caused me to think about the debate on guns in America quite a bit, and parts of both arguments make sense. But in America, our discussions around guns have become intertwined with our discussions around politics. Most people in this debate tend to choose a side, and whatever side that is, we tend to dig our heels in and fight for our position.

While opinions are strongly held, these arguments often lack the fundamental tools of learning. Entrenchment is a natural enemy of curiosity. Maintaining a strong conviction without objective research demonstrates a passive contempt for evidence.

Whether it is the cable news station we watch, the newspapers we read, or the chat rooms we log into, we tend to gravitate to those places where people share our opinions. It's natural, but we risk living in echo chambers where we can only hear what we already know.

What would happen if a contentious issue was examined by someone who gathered all the facts and presented both sides, including the data each side leaves out of the argument? What if, on subjects where conversations can be difficult, there was a guide to a better way to have these conversations? What if the guide was tailored so that you could be prepared to have these conversations with neighbors, colleagues, advocates, and especially children?

It has long been said that information is power. Accuracy brings integrity to that power. Katie Schweit's book leans on her skills as an FBI agent trained to follow the facts no matter where they lead. It taps into her background as a lawyer who can make sense of 200 years of legal decisions. This book draws from her experience as a trainer and coach who understands how both sides of an argument may have merit. Schweit brings together the information and historical context needed to understand the debate on guns in America from a 360 degree view but does so with objectivity and balance. This is not one of the many books that will tell you *what* to think about guns in America, but instead it will tell you *how* to think about guns in America, essential at a time when we all need a better understanding.

John Miller, New York Police Department,
Deputy Commissioner of Intelligence and Counterterrorism, retired

CHAPTER 1

Let's Start Talking With Each Other, Including Kids!

When it comes to guns, we can all agree about one thing … we'll never agree about guns.

Some want no guns, and some want more guns.

Some want less regulation, and some want more regulation.

Most of us are simply too hesitant to discuss the subject.

That's because gun conversations instantly raise the temperature in the room. They pit family members against each other. They turn conversation at a social gathering into heated situations where the loudest voice talks the most.

Wouldn't it be nice if that weren't the case? What if you were armed with information and ideas that turned one-way gun conversations into discussions and mostly friendly debates? The secret sauce? Know your facts and keep your emotions in check.

I can't help you remain calm, but I can arm you with facts and strategies that will help you respond to your finger-wagging friend who is telling you, "Guns don't kill people, people kill people," or "We just need to get rid of all the guns like they did in Australia."

Life's many experiences mold our views, and it's not uncommon to see two people try to have a conversation with only a cursory knowledge of the related facts, and some of those might come from a social media post by someone they don't even know.

MY REASON FOR WRITING THIS BOOK

I've been involved in plenty of gun conversations myself, but I come to the party with an advantage. I spent 20 years as a special agent in the Federal Bureau of Investigation (FBI). Before that, I was a prosecutor in Chicago.

Those last five years in the FBI were spent creating and running the FBI's Active Shooter program, a program focused on researching mass shootings, developing training for law enforcement, and sharing best practices in prevention, response, and recovery. That assignment fell on my shoulders in the weeks following the massacre at the Sandy Hook Elementary School in Connecticut, where 20 children and six women were killed.

I embraced this new challenge to be on the leading edge of understanding and combating the problem. It allowed me to talk to people who were wounded, surgeons who saved lives, mothers who lost children, and law enforcement officers who had seen and then been forced to walk around bodies damaged by high velocity rifle rounds.

When I retired from my FBI executive position in 2017, my mission pivoted from supporting law enforcement to supporting the public. Though I didn't ask for or plan to be an expert in mass shootings, I am one now. I work as a private consultant for companies, organizations, and education-focused groups. I better appreciate the far-reaching impact of these crimes and how they touched so many people in so many ways, permanently. This motivates me daily and fuels me to keep going.

Turning the tide on spiraling firearms violence must begin with respecting each others' choices and working with facts. It must include listening to all voices. It requires an appreciation that gun violence is everyone's problem. And finally, if we think hard enough and talk through the options together, the solutions will come to us.

On my kitchen cupboard, I have a tattered gray file card with a quote typed on it. It so struck me when I read it, that I have left it taped there like an eyesore for six months. As I worked through this book, I saw that card every day as I took out a water glass, a teacup, or a wine glass.

"Sometimes the situation is only a problem because it is looked at in a certain way," it reads. "Looked at in another way, the right course of action may be so obvious that the problem no longer exists."

You may not have heard of him, but let me share a bit about the author of this quote, the expert thinker, Dr. Edward de Bono. Born in Malta, he went on to help establish Cambridge's medical college and was on the faculty of many universities, including Harvard and the University of London. He has several earned and honorary degrees. At university, he was on the canoeing team and played polo. He was once on the short list for the Nobel Prize in Economics.

De Bono died in 2021 at the age of 88. He left behind 85 books; many focus on ways to make people better thinkers. In fact, he believed the practice of thinking should be taught in schools. He preached that no way of looking at a situation was so sacred that it could not be reconsidered. In his book *How to Have a Beautiful Mind*, he said, "A discussion should be a genuine attempt to explore a subject rather than a battle between competing egos."

That's sound advice.

By continuing to explore gun violence another way, I'm confident we'll find those options that will be so obvious the problem soon will no longer exists. Solutions to gun violence are moving targets. What might have worked last year might not work this year or in your town. Continuing the conversation in households, neighborhoods, and communities will provide many solutions if we are willing to see them. Some may be easier than others.

Some ideas discussed in this book are more about growing awareness and are the perfect places to start talking about guns. For example, we can do a better job protecting each other if we know what our role is in preventing gun violence. Discussions can start with what is happening in your own home about when and how to lock up guns and ammunition to keep guns away from children and those contemplating suicide.

Have confidence to speak out freely, even to a spouse or partner who might be lax with gun safety. It's called being an upstander. Ask about firearms in houses where your children might play. Talk to each other and your kids about gun safety.

Becoming more comfortable with these discussions will lead you to other topics.

The last chapters of this book are dedicated to working through more complex ideas to combat gun violence. Some are efforts—laws, policies, rules and habits—many people have worked on for years, and some are ideas developed based on my experiences. Some might be good ideas, but they are only possible if there is a true desire change our course. Some might only work for some groups or communities.

One thing we can be certain of is that if people are afraid to talk about guns, the death toll will continue to rise.

In my book *Stop the Killing, How to End the Mass Shooting Crisis*, I discuss the history of mass shootings and help readers explore the value of a change in policies and procedures in schools and businesses. I detail how to incorporate non-scary safety training into both, even how to talk to kids and learn what to do in a shooting. I focus on providing readers with a roadmap to understand the many aspects of active shooters and mass shootings, including the issues about firearms.

As I have traveled, I find conversations about guns involve a host of opinions and a lot of anger.

Basic debate rules say you should know your opponent's argument better than he or she does. But I've grown to appreciate that some gun owners think they know and understand everything about guns and the Second Amendment, although they do not. And many non-gun owners—as many as two out of three of the American population—have limited knowledge about guns and gun laws, and often are more likely to have been stymied in how they engage in a conversation with a gun owner about reducing gun violence.

ARM YOURSELF WITH FACTS

- For many who own the estimated 400 million firearms in America, guns are a sport, a skill, or maybe just a fun toy for backyard target practice. The Olympics have 15 different competitions involving rifles, shotguns, and pistols, a tradition dating back 100 years. Somewhere around five percent of the country's citizens signed for the 15 million hunting permits issued in 2020, according to the US Fish and Wildlife Service. Tens of thousands more pack their gear in their trunks for a few competitive hours each week of recreational skeet and trap shooting.
- Idle firearms in a home may be legacy items from Grandpa or Grandma, a memory of childhood days with Dad, or perhaps symbols of having proudly served in law enforcement or the military. Most, I say with more hope than belief, are locked securely away or have firing pins removed.
- Most gun owners say they want the gun for protection, but unsecured firearms are one of our most stealth killers in the United States. In 2021, the Centers for Disease Control and

Prevention (CDC) estimated 26,000 people died by firearms suicides. That's more deaths than firearms homicides. Sadly, guns are the most effective means of committing suicide and the largest group making that choice are rural White males.
- Another frightening fact is the 550 people the CDC identified as dying in 2022 from unintentional discharges of firearms, with children under the age of five making up the largest and growing group of victims. In 2020, firearms-related injuries became the leading cause of death among US children and adolescents.

Firearms violence impacts communities differently. The CDC found Blacks are 12 times more likely than Whites and six times more likely than Hispanics to be the victim of a firearms homicide. Based on the CDC's estimate and just comparing two races, for the 20,000 firearm-related homicides in 2021 that would proportionally translate to 1,500 White victims for every 18,000 Black victims.

The last 20 years have also shown us the darker side of gun ownership, such as dead young students in school rooms, murdered parishioners, and massacres at concerts. Many were killed because they were Black, Jewish, transgender, Hispanic, or simply in the wrong place at the wrong time.

WE AGREE ON PLENTY

As divergent as opinions seem on firearms, there are also many areas where more of us agree. Perhaps more than we realize.

In 2022, Gallup asked Americans dozens of questions about firearms, including whether those surveyed owned a firearm, their attitude about firearms laws, their fears involving firearms violence, and their ideas for solutions. Consider these consensus answers about gun purchase limitations. Here are some of the results.

- 92% of those polled favored requiring background checks for all gun sales.
- 77% supported enacting a 30-day waiting period for all gun sales.
- 76% said yes to raising the legal age to purchase certain firearms from 18 to 21.

Were these anti-gun, non-gun owners polled? No. Of those polled, 45 percent indicated they owned guns or had guns in their home or on their property.

While you don't have to agree with these views, remember that seven in 10, or maybe even nine out of 10 people do.

In October 2022, Gallup asked those who own firearms to prioritize the reasons why they do so. A whopping 88 percent placed "protection against crime" first on their list of reasons, up from 63 percent in the 2019 poll. Of those polled, 70 percent also added for target shooting and 56 percent included hunting.

STARTING THE CONVERSATION

If you are asked about firearms violence solutions, don't walk away. Better yet, get the conversation started. We all have so much to learn, and we aren't going to solve this complex situation by keeping our blinders on.

As you engage, listen carefully to not only what is said but how it is said. A conversation with someone might start with a simple question, "Would you ever buy a gun?" or a compound question, "Do you own a gun and why?"

But sometimes people unknowingly hinder or simply cut short productive conversations because they speak only in declaratory statements such as, "Gun violence is an urban problem, not a rural problem." The declaratory statements don't really leave room for conversation. Comments are stated as fact.

Think back to situations you've been in where this has happened and how the frustration is compounded when you know the facts are wrong. You don't want to get into an argument. It's even more challenging when a declaratory statement has a leading question attached to disguise it as a question like, "Guns don't kill people, people kill people, so it doesn't make sense to take away my guns, does it?"

"Guns don't kill people, people kill people."

"I agree with that. The problem that I see is that troubled people with guns kill innocent people. Do you have practical ways to keep guns out of the hands of those troubled people?"

Here are some examples.

If your first volley to a gun owner is that they should give up their guns, remember that many people say they buy guns because it makes them feel safe. It doesn't matter if it does not make you feel safe. And it doesn't even matter if it makes them truly safer because feeling safe and being safe are two different things. Consider that a challenge to gun ownership could be interpreted as asking them to put themselves, their family, and friends at higher risk, or to ask them to set aside their hobbies.

Can you discuss with a gun owner a change you would like to see to keep children safer, or an effort in your family, neighborhood, or town, to bring gun owners and non-gun owners together to share information and show a united front against unsecured guns in homes? Talk together to find other areas of common ground or compromise.

What if you are the gun owner?

If your first volley to a non-gun owner is to say the Second Amendment gives you the absolute right to carry and this is all just a mental health problem, you are missing two areas for common ground. First, you miss a chance to acknowledge their fear and help them understand a bit more about firearms. Second, you miss an opportunity to be honest and acknowledge that the Second Amendment doesn't give unfettered rights and that you do—like the overwhelming number of Americans polled—find some limitations reasonable for a safer society.

Everyone should be advocating for more available and affordable mental health services. See, we agree already! Seeing eye-to-eye in some efforts helps you move to tough conversations about firearms prevention efforts.

It's win-win when the goal is a more informative and calmer conversation. You catch more flies with honey. Can you acknowledge their words may be based on fear about firearms violence and not necessarily a challenge to all lawful gun ownership?

If the starting point is to acknowledge the fear and frustration, then it might be easier to move on to find ways to keep troubled people away from firearms.

Everyone should feel comfortable advocating for less or more regulations or even for ways to reduce or eliminate access to firearms. Skilled advocates for their position go after the facts, not the person.

Remember author Stephen Covey's maxim, "Seek first to understand, then to be understood." And if you aren't a Covey fan, consider the blunter words of author Ernest Hemingway: "When people talk, listen completely."

Some other areas of agreement

In that same 2022 Gallup poll, everyone queried seemed eager for solutions and were willing to support different efforts to reduce firearms violence. Gun owners and non-gun owners alike pointed toward potential common ground.

When asked if they supported "allowing the courts to order the confiscation of guns from those deemed to be a danger to themselves or others," 81 percent of those polled responded yes. When asked if there should be "a ban on the manufacture, possession, and sale of semi-automatic guns, known as assault rifles," 55 percent said yes.

This is a good place to pause and say that though Gallup has been asking this question for years, the language choice makes gun owners cringe. Assault weapon is a subset of semiautomatic rifles, pistols, and shotguns, indicating those with removable magazines we'll say for simplicity's sake. But I think their point is, does the person polled want to see a change regarding semi-automatic rifles or pistols, or assault weapons in general?

Firearms ownership and firearms violence are complicated cousins. This is important to remember when you are a gun owner, and the other person is not, or vice versa. In the heat of the moment, it is easy to forget that we are all on the same side in terms of wanting to resolve gun violence.

OUR OPINIONS ARE OFTEN AS STRONG AS OUR KNOWLEDGE IS WEAK.

I say this from the vantage point of a person who arrived at the FBI academy having only shot a firearm a handful of times before the age of 36. I was a city kid who grew up in a relatively safe area in Michigan. Guns were for my cousins and friends who hunted and shot at targets. I didn't need a gun when I was a prosecutor in Chicago. But I owned several firearms as an FBI agent and became quite proficient in their use.

The falsity of all guns or no guns.

Endless variables impact choices in gun ownership, including where you live in the country, whether you live around people, local and federal laws, and whether your friends have guns. Are you a rancher, a hunter, a retired member of the military, a nurse who works nights in a rough part of town, or someone who thinks it makes you look cool to carry it around?

It's okay if we don't all agree about who should be able to own a gun and under what circumstances. That's what I tell my students at DePaul University College of Law in Chicago. On the first day of our class on the Second Amendment, I remind them the best lawyers can defend an opponent's position from every angle. Author Harper Lee wrote in *To Kill a Mockingbird*, "You never really understand a person until you consider things from his point of view." Only then, I tell my students, can you successfully argue your case in court.

To help understand another's point of view, improve your understanding of the laws and regulations about firearms. That's relatively easy. I'll guide you through where we are now, nationally and locally. Remember, this can change, and local communities can have detailed exceptions to many rules.

Look for the common ground

For example, you could move the conversation to suicide prevention. Suicide is a leading cause of death in the US and about half of recorded suicides in 2022 involved firearms. You could move the conversation to ways to secure firearms in a home, or ways to talk to kids about gun safety.

Gallup pollsters found an overwhelming number of people wanted more done to prevent these deaths, and those polled believed changes in firearms laws and regulations might help. Are you against or an advocate for changes in background check requirements, waiting periods, and the age to purchase a gun? These are good conversations to have.

When chatting, it's okay to ask each other theoretical questions without giving an absolute opinion. This, in fact, might be a more effective conversation technique that encourages discussion without all the defensive posturing required when one feels compelled to justify a firm view. These conversations help us learn more, too. How much do you really know about the background check process other than people are required to fill out a form if they want to buy a gun?

"I don't know anything about guns, and I don't want my kids knowing about guns."

"I appreciate that guns are a scary topic, but the reality is that there are lots of guns in this country. I taught my kids about guns just to make sure they were safe if they ended up around one. I'd be happy to talk with you and your kids about gun safety, or even take you to the range to show you how I use my gun for target practice."

DON'T FORGET THE KIDS!

Hopefully, this book will be a good resource for discussions with kids, even if the many details are too much for them to handle. Kids don't need to know how many people die from firearms violence annually or that firearms are the leading cause of death among children and teens.

But don't count them out of the conversations.

Maybe this is naively controversial to say. But it's best to start the conversation about guns with your own kids before someone else controls that conversation. Guns are part of our culture and entertainment. If you are a family that hunts or shoots for sport, you're likely to have a conversation about gun safety with your child. You tell your children they are not allowed to touch a gun without the permission of an adult or even own a gun by law until they are at least 18 years of age. But does the conversation go beyond that? Are you discussing suicide prevention and talking to your child about what to do when their classmates talk about gun violence? Discuss respecting those who prohibit guns in their home and how to handle it when friends ask to see a gun in your home.

If there are no guns in your house, remember your children are likely to visit a home or place with a gun present. That may occur in a school or at a friend's house. Talk to your kids about gun safety, and I mean more than just saying stay away from guns. If you don't know how to do that, ask a friend who owns guns to talk to your kids with you present.

Kids are fascinated with guns and clinical experiments have shown that many kids will not heed the advice of adults to not touch a gun or even notify an adult when they see a gun. Your gun conversations need to include so much more.

What would you say if a child asked if you have a gun? What would you say if they asked you to let them see it? Would your child be comfortable enough to tell you they saw a gun at someone's house, and what would you do with that information? Run through some answers in your head so you know how to answer truthfully but firmly about your beliefs and how they are based on keeping everyone safe.

Reassure kids routinely that they won't get in trouble for showing you or telling you where they saw a gun. It's the same advice you should give them for warnings about drugs and alcohol. They are most afraid they will get in trouble for tattling when others find out.

Tell them you'll keep them out of it and it's not snitching. It's also incredibly important to convince them they must tell you immediately if someone shows them a gun, talks about getting a gun, seeing a gun, or worse.

Maybe it is an innocent interaction, but either way it provides future opportunities to talk about gun safety. It's also a chance to speak to adults in the homes, businesses, and schools.

Remember, kids have feelings and fears too. Don't hesitate to discuss with your kids how adults and kids alike can get frustrated sometimes and having a gun around can be a dangerous thing. You won't be the only one talking with them, but you want to put yourself in the best spot to be the first one they turn to.

Kids view videos about school shootings and mass shootings on social media feeds. They talk about guns with their friends. Some social media and many websites glorify mass killers. Engage teenagers in conversation about what they see in video gaming and online, encouraging them to tell you or text a tip line if they think someone is making even the smallest threat to commit violence or suicide.

Have them load the tip lines into their contact list. They can just text if they don't want to call. They will worry about getting someone in trouble, but assure them that the police can't arrest someone or get someone in trouble just because they heard some information on a random tip. Police must do some investigating first.

Also, take charge of your children's safety by being comfortable enough to ask other parents if there are guns in their house and if they are all under lock and key. Don't leave this burden on the children, and don't be offended if someone asks you that. Better yet, with the rising fatalities of unintended childhood deaths, make this conversation part of the norm in your community.

Whether or not you have guns, volunteer this information to the parents of children visiting your house, so they are comfortable to tell you the same. Make sure everyone knows the guns are locked up or if they are not.

Imagine what it is like for the loving and doting parents who thought they had successfully secreted a handgun in a high kitchen cupboard, but were called to the 12-year-old's middle school and discovered he had shot and killed a teacher before killing himself. Their friends loved the way he helped the parents in their store. He was a pretty good student and musician, who had friends and hobbies. Yet, he left his parents a letter apologizing for disappointing them. He was a troubled person who had access to a gun.

"I don't want my kid to have to do drills in school for a potential shooting, it's just scary and wrong."

"It is scary, but if we approach it as another aspect of safety drills, like fire and tornado drills, then they just view it as safety training for something that is not likely to happen. Truthfully, I think kids get this better than their parents do."

Talking to Kids About Safety Training at School

Another conversation to have is safety training. Many schools include Run. Hide. Fight. training or some type of training in the event of an active shooter. Even if you don't want your child to have this training and opt out, appreciate that they will still talk about the training at lunch and on the bus with any classmate who attended. Ask them what they have heard and know.

Call your school principal or an administrator or stop by and ask to be briefed on what the training involves and what the kids are told so you know how to lead a conversation with your child.

Are there armed people in the school besides a school resource officer? Ask your child if they know who is armed at school and what others are saying about it. Ask them about the safety drills run in school for fire, tornadoes, active shooters, hurricanes, earthquakes, power outages, and more.

I have spoken to many parents who are afraid of the topic of guns and shy away from any discussion. That approach leaves their kids with all the fear and none of the information. Engaging with kids allows parents to reinforce training and turn the safety training into part of a regular school year.

You may overhear your kids talking about the training or imitating the training. That's okay. They can apply this training to any place they go, whether it is your church or mosque, or the park or library.

If you are mad about safety training and think it's wrong, that's okay. We're all mad that this is the state we are in today. That doesn't take away the need to protect our children from not only the threat of a school shooting but also the FEAR of a school shooting.

We have generations of students impacted by or living through two decades of celebrated school shootings. A senior attending Columbine High School when their shooting occurred in 1999 is at least 40 years old by now. Their kids are now in school or have graduated.

Talking About Toy Guns and Video Games

Parents have often asked me what they should do about a child obsessed with and asking parents to purchase toy guns or shooting video games. There isn't a single or perfect answer to this question. As a parent, I say stick to your guns, no pun intended. If you are determined not to let your five-year-old have a toy gun, a squirt gun, or Nerf gun, say so. Children adapt to the world around them and they will find other things to do. That said, as any parent learns, sometimes a little exposure to something can end an obsession.

It's a different concern if your middle school or teenage child is obsessed with what they can do with a gun, spends time on websites where people are talking about shootings, or photoshops their picture on to images with guns.

If this is happening, it is time to talk to your child and investigate what they are doing. That includes looking at their various online personas—yes, many have more than one. It's equally important you share your concerns with a school counselor, principal, teacher, others who spend time around the child, even law enforcement.

Don't send me hate mail for suggesting this. Parents, understandably, see their children through rose-colored glasses. With firearms the number one killer of teens and kids in the US, don't take a chance that yours might be one of them. Post shooting investigations tell us what parents already know, that kids are good at lying to their parents when they want to hide things like guns and plans for mass murder. As parents, we want to believe them, but as a parent, I followed the adage popularized by former President Ronald Reagan: trust but verify.

The years when teenage anxiety can give way to admiring other school shooters are a tricky time. It's nearly impossible to predict what seemingly happy-go-lucky 10-year-old will a few years later mistakenly believe they can take back control of their fate by killing others.

> **I know we disagree about whether people should be able to own guns, but can we agree to disagree about that and then talk about how we might better tackle some solutions to gun access for those who are in a mental health crisis? To work towards solving gun violence, we have to be able to talk about it.**

CHAPTER 2

The Violence Landscape

WHAT IS A FIREARM?

Firearms are generally placed into the three big categories of shotguns, rifles, and handguns to aid in fitting them neatly into laws, regulations, and rules.

Federal US Code, Title 18, defines the term firearm as "(A) any weapon (including a starter gun) which will or is designed to or may readily be converted to expel a projectile by the action of an explosive; (B) the frame or receiver of any such weapon; (C) any firearm muffler or firearm silencer; or (D) any destructive device. Such term does not include an antique firearm."

Different laws govern other things, such as mines, explosives, bombs, and incendiary devices with larger charges. Consider all the things that accompany gun use too, such as the ammunition, magazines, and scores of items that can modify and enhance a firearm, such as red dot lasers, scopes, suppressors, magnifiers, and light attachments.

It can quickly seem overwhelming to try to understand all aspects of firearms. Automatic and semi-automatic are also two good terms to understand. Both automatic and semiautomatic weapons are firearms that automatically load the next round into the chamber after a trigger pull. Firearms that are automatic, sometimes called fully automatic, fire the loaded ammunition continuously if you are holding the trigger. Semi-automatic rifles and semi-automatic handguns require a trigger pull for each round discharged. In the Las Vegas Live Nation music concert mass shooting, the shooter used an enhancement called a bump stock on his semi-automatic rifles, equipment that accelerated the ability to fire rounds.

Automatic firearms are more strictly regulated, more expensive, and not manufactured or sold generally, so most gun violence involves weapons that are single fire or semi-automatic.

"Why on earth would you own a gun or keep one in your house?"

"I use mine for target practice, a sport I like. But I saw stats that said most people keep them for protection, so when I talk to people who have guns, I also try to remember they want that protection for themselves and their families."

A Gun by any Other Name is Still a Gun.

One of the frequent characterizations repeated in news reports is that a shooter was using an AR-15, or an AR-15 style weapon. I am often asked what this means. Here's some background.

In 1959, the Colt Manufacturing Company bought the patent design and trademark name from the ArmaLite Corporation for a firearm that, four years later, it released as the ArmaLite AR-15, quickly nicknamed the AR-15. The semi-automatic AR-15 was designed, in part, to replicate a fully automatic rifle familiar to the 2.7 million Americans who served during the Vietnam War. Early on, the ArmaLite Corporation had hoped to develop a small-caliber weapon for the US Air Force, but that did not occur, resulting in the Colt purchase. By 1977, the Colt patent had expired but not the trademark, and other firearms manufacturers scrambled to make a near similar weapon but had to use a different name than AR-15, which was still protected.

Coinciding with their decision to change their mission, described in chapter six, the NRA and gun manufacturers were among those aggressively encouraging the purchase of this expanding opportunity to market AR-15-style rifles, touting them as the latest modern sporting rifle. By 2011, Americans had purchased seven million of them, but that was just the beginning. Now, the National Shooting Sports Foundation estimates Americans have spent $1 billion to own more than 20 million AR-15-style rifles. Many reside in gun lockers as trophies, and others are perched, loaded, in bedroom closets, beside beds, in kitchens and by front doors.

THE VIOLENCE LANDSCAPE

To compare firearms violence to the broader landscape of death, let's step back even further.

In 2020, the CDC identified the leading causes of death in the US as diseases of the heart (696,000), followed by malignant neoplasms such as cancers (602,000), and COVID-19 (350,000). Unintentional injuries causing death are bundled together and accounted for another 200,000 deaths that same year from a variety of means, most notably unintended falls (42,000), motor vehicle accidents (40,000), and unintentional poisonings (87,000). Chronic diseases and health challenges, such as kidney and liver diseases and diabetes, make the list.

Then the CDC categorizes a block of intended acts causing death, grouping together these incidents whether they involved a gun, an intentional car crash, a jump from a bridge, or other means.

So, deaths involving firearms and other means first appears 12th on the CDC's list, categorized as intentional self-harm, also known as suicide. Of the nearly 46,000 suicides documented in 2020, about half of those involved the use of a firearm.

For many years, the CDC has also tracked the per capita rate of firearms mortality in each state, which allows for an apples-to-apples comparison of the risk to citizens of each state who are exposed to firearms by any means.

Here is the CDC list in rank order from the most dangerous to the least dangerous state. The CDC has calculated the death rate, taking population into consideration, of all deaths accounted for with a firearm. This is a great way to understand an individual's overall risk from firearms violence, whether the person is killed by their own hand or someone else.

CDC data for 2020 shows that the highest risk is in Mississippi and then in Louisiana. From there, in decreasing order, Wyoming, Missouri, Alabama, Alaska, New Mexico, Arkansas, South Carolina, Tennessee, Montana, Oklahoma, Kentucky, West Virginia, Georgia, Idaho, Indiana, Nevada, Kansas, Arizona, North Carolina, Colorado, Ohio, Michigan, and Delaware.

Following on, these 25 states proceed in rank order down to the safest state in the union when it comes to firearms violence: Texas, Illinois, North Dakota, Florida, Utah, South Dakota, Pennsylvania, Maryland, Virginia, Oregon, Wisconsin, Vermont, Iowa, Washington, Maine, Nebraska, New Hampshire, Minnesota, California, Connecticut, New York, Rhode Island, New Jersey, Massachusetts, and Hawaii.

Firearms Violence

Firearms are the most effective means to death, whether by homicide or suicide.

In 2020, just over 45,000 people died in a firearm-related death in the US, according to the most recent data available from the CDC. This includes about 25,000 suicides and about 20,000 homicides. From

2019 to 2020, the firearm homicide rate increased about 35 percent, the highest recorded in over 25 years. Of all homicides, 79 percent involved firearms.

Before you use these numbers, consider that the raw numbers don't consider the nation's growing population. On a per capita basis, there were 13.6 gun deaths per 100,000 people in 2020, well below the peak of 16.3 gun deaths per 100,000 people in 1974.

Violence, whether or not with a firearm, generally fits into one of two categories: impulsive or reactive, and predatory or planned.

Impulsive or reactive violence is an emotionally based response to a perceived and imminent threat. This might be a violent response by somebody who believes they are going to be raped or killed, or it could occur when the subject is intending to commit a crime or another type of violence.

The second kind of violence—predatory or planned violence—is most often seen in premeditated murders, suicides, acts of terrorism, and murder-suicide incidents. Planned violence is the basis for targeted violence, including active shooter incidents and other mass shootings that occur in public and in private spaces.

Though these planned shootings are often called mass shootings in news stories, the causes of the shootings and who are potentially in danger are very different. Consider who is in danger when a gang member conducts a drive-by shooting at a rival gang member's home or when a woman and her four children are killed in their home by an irate domestic abuser.

The destructive impact of domestic violence is discussed in more detail in chapter nine.

Some of the FBI's research during the past 10 years has focused on active shooters, that is, the planned public shootings where the shooter is on the move and where both the police and civilian response can impact, and hopefully reduce, the number of casualties. These are the incidents the media disproportionately covers.

Though more firearms violence involves conflicts between people in their own homes, the public killings are the incidents that dig our heels into the ground and prompt us to take our stand on firearms.

The FBI's research on active shooters was conducted to better understand the planned violence that occurs in more populated and public spaces, such as concerts, office buildings, and schools. These types of shootings do not discriminate by location and that enhances our it-could-happen-anywhere fear. Even with the first research done by the FBI, researchers found active shooters incidents occurred in 40 of the 50 states and the District of Columbia, painting this as a truly American problem.

The FBI's research released in 2014 on 160 active shooters incidents showed:

- 45.6% struck at a place of business
- 24.4% in educational settings
- 10% in government buildings
- 9.4% in open spaces
- 4.4% in residential settings
- 3.8% in houses of worship
- 2.5% in health care facilities

A 2022 US Department of Agriculture annual report on rural America found 48 percent of those polled said they were very or somewhat worried someone in their family would become a victim of a mass shooting.

Now let's match that against reality. Though nearly half of the

Americans polled were very or somewhat worried someone in their family would become a victim of a mass shooting, these types of shootings account for less than one percent of all firearm deaths when excluding domestic violence incidents, according to the Johns Hopkins Center for Gun Violence Solutions.

A focus on mass shooting is understandable. They shock us. Like it or not, news agencies and streaming services consistently devote more time to these types of shootings than to the daily violence that occurs across America. They do this because that's what we click on and watch.

> "Give me one good reason why anyone should be able to own a rifle?"

> "That's a fair question. For me, there are two main reasons that I and many of my friends own rifles. The first is hunting. People hunt wild hogs, deer, bear, and wolves with rifles primarily because they can hit a target that is further away. There are millions of hunters in this country who enjoy this activity and handguns are difficult to use for this kind of hunting. I also know simple target shooting is very popular with rifles."

ARE WE LOSING THE BATTLE?

I've spent a decade focused on the threat of mass shootings, but as a career FBI agent and a former Chicago prosecutor, I appreciate there is a much larger landscape to crime and gun violence.

Around the country, people often ask, are we losing the battle for a less violent world?

No, I don't think so.

In both Gallup polls and Pew Research Center surveys, Americans routinely respond that they believe the current year was more violent compared to the year before. Respondents believe violent crime has steadily increased since 2008. But let's look at the crime trends by the numbers to see how crime has changed through the decades.

The Department of Justice collects data from the nation's 18,000 law enforcement departments and releases an annual tally known as the Uniform Crime Reporting (UCR). The most common statistic from the UCR is the homicide rate. But the UCR tracks a wider set of crimes it calls violent crimes that are composed of these offenses: murder and nonnegligent manslaughter, forcible rape, robbery, and aggravated assault. These are the crimes that involve force or a threat of force.

Looking at the past 20 years of this data, URC information shows that in 1993, police reported 747 violent crimes for every 100,000 people in the country. Since that time, that number has dropped steadily to a low of 361 violent crimes reported in 2014. That's more than a 50 percent decrease. In the ensuing years, the number has risen slightly. It was 395 in 2021, but that is still a dramatic decrease from the previous two decades.

Violent crime overall is down for a variety of reasons. Two reasons include more police on the streets and more criminals in jail. FBI records show steady decreases in burglaries, robberies, car thefts, and other crimes.

So, in contrast to what you hear, overall violent crime isn't skyrocketing. But even that is not the whole story. Certain crimes are trending up. Most notably, FBI records show a dramatic increase in recorded murders, with a 29 percent increase from 2019 to 2020 alone.

Understanding the vast array of available data is a challenge, but view the information as a way to inform your discussions about gun violence solutions. More information can be found by looking at the FBI online info regarding UCR and the companion data in its National Incident-Based Reporting System (NIBRS). NIBRS gathers data on crime trends.

We can do better. Many still do not feel safe, and the shifting increase in the murder rate and constant chatter on the news and social media leave us all jumpy. Numbers are tools to help us understand, but by themselves they can't impact the gun violence landscape in the US. Appreciating the policies, politics, and laws surrounding firearms through the years can aid in our efforts to have productive discussions and find the most promising pathways in that landscape that can lead to a safer community.

> **I know we disagree about the right to carry guns concealed or in public, but can we agree to disagree about that and then talk about ideas to keep people safe in public spaces?**

CHAPTER 3

Regulating Gun Purchases

GUNS FROM THE BEGINNING

In the beginning, what we now think of as firearms were initially handmade and often expensive.

Their genesis can be found in the ninth century invention of gunpowder by the Chinese and the time around the 11th century when the Chinese designed handheld devices using a gunpowder explosion to propel objects forward. These had humble beginnings, propelling objects only a few feet forward. Centuries of warfare that followed included castle attacks with catapults, and cannons first on land and then on sea modeled after the Chinese hand cannons.

The crude and refined permutations appeared simultaneously in different parts of the world from the 10th to 15th centuries. The standardization of ideas, styles, and techniques in the 19th century are the origins of the thousands of varieties of handguns, shotguns, and rifles we are currently familiar with.

Today, anyone over the age of 21 can buy a variety of handguns, shotguns, and rifles in the US. Federal law restricts the purchase of handguns to those 21 or older though, as discussed in chapter seven, a recent US Supreme Court case may call into question the constitutional support for that cutoff.

In fact, less gun regulation was in play when America was

discovered, and in the century after the US declared its independence. Gun laws focused through the centuries more on where guns could be carried in a town, for example, to prevent drunken gunfights in a theater or saloon or an accidental discharge in a church or school. Handmade guns and hand-filled ammunition were expensive, inherently limiting who could use a firearm for sport.

Chapter six provides a more expansive view of the laws surrounding firearms. But let's start with this primer.

It wasn't until the 1930s that federal laws truly began to limit who could and could not buy a gun and what they could buy. Limits were established to prohibit sales to felons and fugitives. Laws created regulations for the purchase of a number of items that could discharge explosives devises, including silencers/suppressors, fully automatic firearms (e.g. machine guns), rifles with barrels less than 16 inches or an overall length of 26 inches, shotguns with barrels less than 18 inches or an overall length less than 26 inches, destructive devices (e.g. grenades, bombs), and dangerous items in a category called Any Other Weapons (e.g. pen guns, umbrella and cane guns).

The Gun Control Act of 1968 expanded prohibitions to include anyone who might be an "unlawful user or addicted to marijuana or any depressant or stimulant drug."

To streamline the process, the act also established a standardized application process. Akin to the Internal Revenue Service's annual tax filing standard forms of 1040 and 1040EZ, the law mandated that potential firearms purchasers fill out a standard form, 4473, that details their background. Some purchasers know this document by a nickname, the yellow sheet, the form often handed to them on a clipboard.

Following many years of debate after the attempted assassination of President Ronald Reagan, Congress passed the bipartisan Brady Handgun Violence Prevention Act of 1993 to manage how Federal

Firearms Licensees (FFLs) could sell firearms. The Brady Act, as it is known, directed the creation of the National Instant Criminal Background Check System (NICS) to standardize the way FFLs evaluate sales to unlicensed individuals.

NICS is managed by the FBI, and each state performs nuanced background checks using NICS and other state resources.

The three-page 4473 form lists a dozen reasons an FFL must decline a sale. Reasons aside, merchant FFLs, as private business owners, can refuse a sale for any reason, without explaining their decision. Most FFLs I've spoken with say they are comfortable refusing a sale for reasons expressed as "he didn't seem right" to "he didn't know what he was doing," or "he looked nervous." Dealing with gun sales every day, dealers often say they can "just tell."

Most handguns cost in the hundreds of dollars, with many shotguns and rifles starting at more than $1,000. High-quality competition weapons are the most expensive, but you can still buy what has turned out to be the Toyota Corolla of shotguns, a Remington 870, for about half of that.

Purchases require payment of taxes and a background check. In some states, a carry permit is required by a local jurisdiction, all adding another five percent to 10 percent to the base cost. Hearing protection and eye protection are a must for most visitors to an indoor range that charges a fee to shoot. Magazines, gun cleaning supplies, and ammunition are also a must. A way to safely lock up and store firearms is necessary. If you will wear the handgun on your body, you need a high-quality holster. Gun sellers with an FFL are allowed to ship guns for a fee.

NICS DETAILS

The FBI and state law enforcement officials began performing NICS checks in 1998 in cooperation with the Bureau of Alcohol, Tobacco, Firearms and Explosives (ATF), and have performed more than 412 million checks to date. During that time, NICS checks have resulted in the denial of about two million transactions, with a current denial rate of just over one percent.

Some news reports exaggerate the number of denials, with one even claiming the FBI "admits" 90 percent of its denials are in error. But FBI data is published annually, including statistics that show 1.1 million, half of the denials, were based on prior qualifying criminal convictions, with other denials occurring when NICS checks found 264,000 were convicted of a qualifying domestic violence law or a were under orders from a domestic violence restraining order, 220,000 were fugitives sought on outstanding warrants, 213,000 were unlawful users of controlled substances, 134,000 were prohibited from a purchase because of their state law, 115,000 had criminal charges pending, and 73,000 had disqualifying mental health adjudications imposed.

Seeking to use this information to aid law enforcement, Republicans have led efforts to require the FBI to inform Immigration and Customs Enforcement and other agencies if it appears a noncitizen is trying to obtain a firearm. Since the inception of NICS, the FBI reports that 45,000 illegal or unlawful aliens have tried to purchase a gun.

FFLs can contact NICS by telephone, or other electronic means, and obtain information immediately indicating whether the transfer of a firearm would violate federal or state law. In 2021, the FBI reported that 88 percent of all FFL checks were done electronically, or by NICS E-Check, as it is called.

The background includes a search through more than 115 million entries in data bases that house information on individuals with criminal histories, those with outstanding warrants for arrest, individuals subject to protection orders, those who have threatened harm to law enforcement, firearms traffickers, and non-US citizens who have tried to buy firearms.

Most checks are completed in minutes, but missing information—such as the result of a felony charge—can prevent a quick return. All checks are categorized as "proceed," "delay," or "deny." The FBI's 2021 annual report on NICS checks indicated that each year, 400,000 to 500,000 checks cannot be completed within the three days allowed for the background check. In those instances, FFL may, but is not required, to sell the firearm to the seller.

During the COVID-pressured surge in sales in 2020, the general counsel for the National Shooting Sports Foundation, Larry Keane, issued a public plea to FFL holders to hold off on transferring a gun to a potential buyer. There's no way to know if this occurred, but he told USA Today in May 2020 that "dealers have offered no resistance to the group's recommendation."

As of December 31, 2021, the FBI reported that the NICS Section supported 50,588 FFLs conducting business in 31 states, five US territories, and the District of Columbia.

An alternative method of checking before a gun sale was explained by the FBI in its 2021 annual report:

> Certain state-issued firearm permits, such as carry concealed weapon permits and permits to purchase, may be qualified by ATF as permits that may be used by the FFL, at their discretion, in lieu of a NICS background check. The transferee must still complete the ATF Form 4473. In addition to meeting the conditions required by state law to qualify for one of these alternate permits, the applicant must pass a NICS background check as part of the permit-issuing/renewal process. The state

> agency responsible for issuing the ATF-qualified alternate permit conducts the NICS check and determines if the subject is eligible, based on federal and state firearm laws. When attempting to obtain a firearm through an FFL, an individual's presentation of a valid alternate permit, issued within the past five years, precludes the need for the FFL to initiate the otherwise required NICS background check for the permit holder. Again, an FFL is not required to accept such permit in lieu of a NICS background check. The renewal of an alternate permit requires a NICS background check as part of the permit process. In addition, when authorized by state law, a NICS background re-check may be conducted by the issuing agency at any time between the time of issuance and the date of renewal for any firearm permit holder. Such rechecks are referred to as "revocation" checks and are conducted by issuing agencies to determine if the permit holder remains eligible to possess the firearm permit. Twenty-five states have at least one ATF-qualified alternate permit.

Though the NICS system does not retain information on background checks performed, FFLs must retain the background check paperwork they collect for a certain period, giving the ATF and other investigators some potential leads if a gun is used in a crime.

CARRYING FIREARMS

Buying a gun and carrying it around are two different things.

Before getting into an argument with your cousin about what is legal or not legal, I'd suggest you look up the local laws. State laws are searchable via the internet and so are local laws.

Call your local police non-emergency number with specific

questions before you make assumptions. The right to carry a firearm some place may be limited if you are headed to a park, school, religious facility, and public building. Nearly all laws allow private property owners to prohibit guns on their property.

If you are traveling, make sure you know what the laws are in the states in which you plan to travel. You also can start the easy way by picking up a copy of *Traveler's Guide to Firearm Laws of the Fifty States*, a booklet released every year by J. Scott Kappas. As best as he is able, Kappas identifies changes in laws state by state and explains terms such as concealed carry, open carry, and how states define self-defense.

It's not a replacement for looking at the laws, but the plain language in the book is a good resource for the unsuspecting gun carrier who thinks it is okay to carry on school grounds, in a park, between states, and recommends what to do in a hotel.

"I think we shouldn't allow concealed carry."

"I respect that, it's just that that's the law right now here, and each community is setting its own standards, so you can work to change the law if you feel that strongly about it. Have you spoken to your congress people and local representatives?"

GUN SALES

In our first century, gun purchases, ownership, and registrations were not tracked in any significant way, though many towns prohibited guns in certain areas, and some even required visitors to check their gun with the local authorities upon arrival in town.

As the 1900s approached, government entities began to impose more limitations on the ability to carry guns or own one without a concealed carry permit. Gun purchases became more of a man's game and gun purchases increased. A National Institute of Justice survey in 1994 showed Americans owned 192 million firearms. According to the ATF, by the end of 2000 that number had risen to 259 million, and then 294 million by 2007.

In the US, men are roughly twice as likely as women to own a gun, at 43 percent to 22 percent. Gun ownership among women has increased from the low teens to more than 20 percent over the past 15 years, while it has remained in the low to mid-40s among men during the same period.

The year after the 1999 massacre at Columbine High School, Americans bought an estimated 7.5 million guns. That number stayed relatively steady until 2007, the year of the massacre on the Virginia Tech campus. From that point forward, gun sales began to rise, with sales estimates ranging between 10 to 16 million annually in the succeeding decade. Once thought to be leveling off, an estimated 42.5 million guns were sold in 2020 and 2021, according to Small Arms Analytics and Forecasting.

In its 2022 annual report, the FBI noted that the COVID pandemic and unrest in the past couple of years has resulted in a record number of NICS checks, month after month.

Why the increase? Many things can impact gun sales in the US. Some reasons are actual threats to safety and others are perceived threats to safety. Those years, 2009–2022, included the pandemic, a Black Democratic president, a siege on the US Capitol, Black Lives Matter marches and protests, supply chain challenges, the Uvalde Elementary School Shooting in Texas, the Marjory Stoneman Douglas High School shooting in Florida, and a series of other events. Consider too the natural disasters of massive forest fires, multiple tornados hitting cities, and devastating hurricanes pummeling the south and eastern parts of the country.

Demand Shock

Firearms manufacturers understand their business. They know anything that makes citizens more afraid may translate into increased demand. These incidents cause what economists call a demand shock to the industry, which drives sales up or down. In this case, these events caused dramatic increases in sales.

That brings us to the present day. Though sales are still more than twice what they were in 2000, industry forecasters anticipate a leveling off for sales at pre-pandemic numbers.

The NRA's Institute for Legislative Action stated enthusiastically in its January 2023 newsletter that "it is possible that the final tally [for 2022] will exceed 15-million-gun sales for the year." Some other estimates I've seen put that number at 18 million.

What the Market will Bear

With an estimated 400 million plus guns in the US, it's fair to ask if the market is or will ever be saturated? The answer might be no because events keep causing demand shock. The answer might be no for other reasons. Just like new cars and computers, manufacturers offer new styles and features each year to lure new buyers. Aggressive sales to women have expanded sales.

Consider the impact when, in 2022, the US House of Representatives passed legislation seeking to ban certain types of assault rifles that was doomed to fail without matching support in the Senate. This no doubt increased demand by those who didn't appreciate the legislation was dead on arrival. Sales were also impacted by other things like the 2022 firearms legislative package signed into law by President Biden, as well as the US Supreme Court's decision impacting the individual right to carry a firearm.

However, it's also worth considering that the overwhelming number of people who are buying guns already own other guns. A study published in 2017 by the Russell Sage Foundation found that half of America's gun stock, at the time approximately 130 million guns, was owned by approximately 14 percent of gun owners.

The Background Check Debate

How many were sold for sure in 2022 or other years? We don't know. The major reason we don't know how many guns are sold or even in circulation is the way gun sales and existing guns are counted. Or rather, how they are not counted.

The FBI's NICS checks just record how many times an FFL sent an application through its system. Most states don't require NICS checks on private sales, and plenty of states allow those with concealed carry licenses to buy guns without a check.

No federal background checks are required on gun sales between two individuals. It surprises me how many people do not know this and mistakenly believe there is some big federal gun registration database.

Gun tracing wears out more shoe leather than computer time. When a gun is found at the scene of a crime, the ATF's National Tracing Center (NTC) reaches back to the gun manufacturer to see where the firearm was originally placed into the market through wholesale and retail distributors. From there, investigators reach out to the involved FFLs, if they are still in business, to see if they can gain information about a potential purchaser. If that happens, then investigators begin the sometimes-arduous task of knocking on doors to see where the gun might have traveled.

When I was an FBI agent in Wisconsin, I was given a lead to

interview the original owner of a gun used in a murder in Chicago. He was shocked to discover this as he explained that he had sold the gun to a friend and had no idea what happened to it after that.

Things get more harried when the FFL is no longer in business. If an FFL goes out of business, they are required by a 1968 law to provide their paper records to the ATF. Finding information in those records can be time consuming and ridiculously tedious. A strong lobbying effort by the NRA, gun manufactures, and others created financial challenges and other roadblocks to smooth operations. For example, the ATF is kept from being able to digitize their records.

Yes, hundreds of millions of records, ATF acknowledges, must be hand sorted to find potential gun sales. When time is of the essence in a criminal investigation, warehouses that look like the last scene of *Raiders of the Lost Ark* are a daunting site to visit.

A 2017 Harvard study found one in five guns were sold privately, without a background check. Some refer to these sales as utilizing the "gun show loophole" and are fighting for legislation to require every transaction to include a background check. I put this term in quotes because this is a very loaded term that does not mean what many people think it means.

I live two miles from a location that bills itself as having the largest gun show in the nation four times a year. At that gun show, FFLs come to sell their products as do other individuals, including some non-FFLs who want to sell firearms. When those guns are sold, no background check is done. This is the genesis of the term "gun show loophole."

What gun control advocates really mean is that they would like to add background checks to any gun sale, private sales, and FFL sales alike. One study on deaths related to weapons sold at gun shows in California and Texas by non-FFLs (so no background check was done) found no evidence that gun shows lead to substantial increases in either gun homicides or suicides or reduce the number of firearms-related deaths. Though some gun show sellers are not FFLs, an unknown and likely larger number of gun sales occur between private individuals in garages and parking lots and homes, which is perfectly legal.

When that gun show occurs near my home, it is the transactions between the occupants in the hundreds of cars in the parking lot that gets my attention.

"Passing gun laws is the beginning of the slippery slope towards taking all our guns away, don't you think?"

"We have millions of guns in this country, so that's not really a realistic fear, but I appreciate that you might be tired of hearing it and you just don't want anyone messing with your guns. It is frustrating that gun violence involves a small number of people, but changes in laws impact law-abiding gun owners. If not gun regulations, do you have some other ideas that might help?"

Sellers Beware!

Every potential seller should be aware that if they knowingly sell a gun to a prohibited person, they are opening themselves up to potential criminal charges. In addition, several states have more restrictive laws on gun transfers, some requiring steps to register or conduct a background check before a sale: my state, Virginia, among them.

The ATF's website offers an annual update of state laws and published ordinances, so you can look up the specific laws in your state.

No matter where you live, one way to protect yourself when selling or transferring a gun is to have a background check run on the purchaser. It's relatively easy. FFLs, found anywhere guns are sold, can run a background check for a modest fee, capped at $15 in Virginia. FFLs know the laws of the state and can explain them. FFLs have electronic systems on site and uneventful purchases allow people to walk out with their purchase immediately unless the shop has a state law with other requirements.

The 2022 annual NICS report by the FBI identified 56,000 private sale NICS background checks in 2020, and 208,000 in 2021, a notable rise.

If you have a gun you don't want in your home, law enforcement agencies in your area will take the gun and dispose of it. Just call the non-emergency number of your state, county, city, or tribal law enforcement agency for help.

Who is on the Prohibited List?

The federal list of who cannot buy a gun is worth reviewing. The prohibited list for gun purchases includes anyone who:

- Has been convicted in any court of a crime punishable by imprisonment for a term exceeding one year—18 U.S.C. § 922(g)(1).
- Is a fugitive from justice—18 U.S.C. § 922(g)(2).
- Is an unlawful user of or addicted to any controlled substance—18 U.S.C. § 922(g)(3).
- Has been adjudicated as mentally defective or committed to a mental institution—18 U.S.C. § 922(g)(4).
- Is illegally or unlawfully in the United States—18 U.S.C. § 922(g)(5).

- Has been discharged from the Armed Forces under dishonorable conditions—18 U.S.C. § 922(g)(6).
- Having been a citizen of the United States, has renounced US citizenship—18 U.S.C. § 922(g)(7).
- Is subject to a court order that restrains the person from harassing, stalking, or threatening an intimate partner or child of such intimate partner—18 U.S.C. § 922(g)(8).
- Has been convicted in any court of a misdemeanor crime of domestic violence (MCDV)—18 U.S.C. § 922(g)(9).
- Is under indictment/charged in a criminal information charging document by a prosecutor for a crime punishable by imprisonment for a term exceeding one year—18 U.S.C. § 922(n).

The number of denials for most categories is detailed earlier in the chapter with the exception of denials based on federally denied persons (6,400), dishonorably discharged persons from the military (1,700), and those who renounced their US citizenship (116).

BREAKING NEWS

As I write this, courts are analyzing these limitations, taking into consideration the US Supreme Court's decision in the summer of 2022. In November 2022, for example, a federal district court judge in Texas found a state law unconstitutional that was designed to keep firearms out of the hands of a potentially dangerous intimate partner. The law would prohibit someone from possessing a weapon if a court found they were a potential threat to an intimate partner.

Last year, Illinois court rulings set the stage for a potential Illinois Supreme Court decision on the state's Protect Illinois Communities Act which, among other things, prohibits the manufacture or possession of semiautomatic handguns and rifles. The law also requires those who own the guns to register them with the state police by January 1, 2024. Challengers to the law claim they are denied equal protection under the law because the law exempts certain classes of people, such as retired police officers, law enforcement, and correction officers. Illinois is one of eight states, along with Washington D.C., which have passed similar laws.

"I like the way the UK has laws that require people to get a license to carry a gun. That includes doing a background check that is more extensive than in the United States. You have to be interviewed and others must vouch for you."

"I don't want to get a license and have a background check done. That invades my privacy."

"I appreciate your concern, but we get licenses to drive a car or pilot a plane. The background interviews in Europe are designed to identify people who may have mental wellness issues, temper issues, or other problems. It's worth giving up a bit of freedom to find those people who maybe shouldn't be allowed to own guns. What do you think?"

THE MARIJUANA DEBATE

To purchase a firearm from a licensed dealer, purchasers must indicate on their federal form 4473 that they are not "an unlawful user of, or addicted to, marijuana or any depressant, stimulant, narcotic drug, or any other controlled substance." The form warns that "the use or possession of marijuana remains unlawful under Federal law regardless of whether it has been legalized or decriminalized for medicinal or recreational purposes in the state where you reside."

As more states legalize uses for marijuana, FFLs need direction on interpreting what appears to be conflicting laws. In September 2011, the ATF issued guidance to licensed firearms dealers reminding them that any marijuana use or possession, even the disclosure of a medical marijuana card, evidenced a prohibition on the sale of a gun through a dealer.

In 2022, hoping to discuss, if not resolve, this growing conflict, President Biden asked the Department of Health and Human Services and Department of Justice (DOJ) to evaluate the Schedule 1 controlled substance status of marijuana. The US Food and Drug Administration (FDA), which is part of Department of Health and Human Services (HHS), was specifically tapped to participate because it has the authority to approve drugs for medicinal use.

As often occurs before legislative or executive actions are taken in Washington, D.C., Congress asked its Congressional Research Service (CRS) to provide a brief description of the facts and issues involved. In its October 2022 report, the CRS noted that federal and state policy conflicts had created eligibility questions on a wide array of matters ranging from visa applications to employment efforts, to housing and food assistance eligibility.

In its conclusion, the CRS indicated that Congress itself could change the schedule status of marijuana or remove it altogether by simply amending the Controlled Substance Act (CSA). The CRS also opined that the Biden Administration on its own, through the FDA process, could move marijuana down or remove it altogether from the schedule of controlled substances.

I found this part of the CRS report somewhat illuminating in that it demonstrates an unwillingness to change the law despite the reality, for example, that a couple dozen states have laws that allow the use of medical marijuana, and growing research shows the potential for therapeutic applications.

Currently, 21 states and Washington, D.C. have legalized the recreational use of marijuana. And together, 38 states and Washington, D.C., have passed laws allowing medical use of the drug.

Political will, perhaps not surprisingly, seems to be the driver of change. Until either Congress or the administration chooses to act, gun buyers and FFLs will continue to dance to this background challenge.

THE GHOST GUN CHALLENGE

Privately made firearms (PMFs) have been aptly nicknamed ghost guns because they do not carry a serial number and do not fit the historic federal definition of a firearm. Firearms are made of several parts that can be interchanged and modified easily. The main body of the firearm, called a frame or receiver, historically was the only part of a gun where manufacturers would leave an identifying serial number. Today, anyone with the right 3D printer can make a frame, and a quick online search shows where to have one mailed to you. No serial number, perfectly legal. Frame in hand, anyone can buy barrels, trigger components, and other parts separately, and, with a few hours, persistence, and a YouTube video, bingo, a gun is in hand. Teenagers are doing it in their garage.

To manage the problem, the definition of a firearm was changed in 2022. This now allows law enforcement to regulate certain homemade firearms as they would any other firearm.

In announcing the change, the ATF noted the dramatic increase in the use of these guns for criminal activity and sale by gun traffickers. In

2016, the ATF responded to 1,758 reports of suspected PMFs. In 2021, that number had risen to 19,344. From January 2016 to December 2021, the 45,240 reports involved 692 homicide or attempted homicide investigations.

> **I know we disagree about many aspects of the Second Amendment, but can we agree to disagree about that and talk about some ideas to end gun violence with our existing laws?**

CHAPTER 4

The Founding Fathers, Militias, and Guns Worldwide

THE SECOND AMENDMENT'S TWENTY-SEVEN WORDS

At a mere twenty-seven words, the US Constitution's Second Amendment is half the length of the important Fourth Amendment, a prohibition against unreasonable search and seizure.

> A well regulated Militia, being necessary to the security of a free State, the right of the people to keep and bear Arms shall not be infringed.

Scores of scholars have opined about the collective minds of the Founding Fathers as the leaders drafted, rejected, amended, and ultimately agreed upon our country's three foundational documents: the Declaration of Independence, signed July 4, 1776; the Constitution, ratified in 1788; and the Bill of Rights, ratified in 1791.

The Declaration did not mention gun rights when it was signed. Only the Constitution and the Bill of Rights discuss guns, and then only in relation to military activities. At the time, the US military was primarily made up of the state militias that supplemented a minimal standing national army.

Little discussion was recorded about standing armies or state militias during debates about the Declaration of Independence. But 11 years later, over four hot and humid months in Philadelphia, the debates over the drafting of the US Constitution shed some light on the founders' thinking.

"The Second Amendment was written to protect citizens against a tyrannical federal government. Don't you believe in the Constitution? I should be able to carry any gun I want without a permit."

"I believe that's not a realistic fear, but my concern is that carrying a gun in public concealed is dangerous. I hear news stories about tempers flaring and shootings happening at bars, in stores, and in parks. When a gun is pulled to resolve an argument in public, that puts so many more people in danger."

It's All About Militias.

The draft Constitution explicitly granted Congress the power to call up state militias. This power, stated in Article 1, Section 8, gives Congress authorization to raise and support armies, as well as "provide for calling forth the Militia to execute the Laws of the Union, suppress Insurrections and repel Invasions."

Giving states the authority to appoint officers to oversee these militias was an effort to appease those states that feared they would lose control of their militias. The debate was not theoretical. Having just wrestled independence from a country with a military ever ready to protect the monarchy, many feared a centralized military could be used against the states in times of unrest. History buffs will note this is exactly what happened during the Civil War.

Trying to dissuade the framers from rejecting strong federal armies, Founding Fathers Alexander Hamilton, John Jay, and James Madison wrote 85 essays over a period of seven months that appeared in various New York newspapers. The essays are known as The Federalist Papers.

Hamilton argued that a strong military would solve a future problem of under-funded state militias. He wrote of those compelled to deploy with insufficient or various types of guns and ammunition. He had seen those challenges firsthand, working beside General Washington during the Revolutionary War.

"If a well-regulated militia be the most natural defense of a free country, it ought certainly to be under the regulation and at the disposal of that body which is constituted the guardian of the national security," Hamilton wrote in Federalist No. 29. But Virginian and fellow Founding Father George Mason led the opposition for strong federal control, refusing to sign the Constitution and discouraging states from ratifying it unless a bill of rights was adopted at the same time. To temper that concern, Founding Father James Madison pointed out, in Federalist No. 46, that the many numbers of state militia would always outweigh the number of federal regular troops. In a prescient thought, he added that Americans were already better armed than the people of almost every other nation.

The result was a 4,400-word Constitution signed in 1787 with little or no mention of individual rights, including the right of gun ownership.

During this time, firearms were a necessary tool for survival. Scarce resources were more easily attainable from nature or hostile native with a gun in hand. American historian Richard Hofstadter once opined that obtaining firearms proved to be a pivotal factor in the victory during the Revolutionary War.

The Bill of Seventeen, er, 10, Rights

At the First Congress in 1789, George Mason proposed a 17-point Bill of Rights, which included a version of what became the Second Amendment. Those opposed to the amendments noted that many state constitutions already had in place an assortment of these rights, including protections for individuals to bear arms to defend their family and home—among them Pennsylvania and North Carolina.

Many argued that the US Constitution only grants specific rights, and all others would be left to the states. Many historians, in fact, generally found the amendments to be form without substance.

The National Constitution Center, a think tank and museum in Philadelphia, described the Second Amendment this way:

> The Second Amendment conceded nothing to the Anti-Federalists' desire to sharply curtail the military power of the federal government, which would have required substantial changes in the original Constitution. Yet the Amendment was easily accepted because of widespread agreement that the federal government should not have the power to infringe on the right of the people to keep and bear arms, any more than it should have the power to abridge the freedom of speech or prohibit the free exercise of religion.

For the Southern states, the need to control their militias was the practical focus of the debates. Representatives from slave states feared that federal control of state militias would pull resources from the militias' primary mission-slave patrols. These patrols were the earliest police forces in the South, Chelsea Hansen wrote for the National Law Enforcement Museum in a blog entitled, "Slave Patrols, An Early Form of American Policing." These patrols were tasked with maintaining slave discipline outside the courts, hunting down runaway slaves, and "providing a form of organized terror to deter slave revolts." After two years of debate, and with enough state representatives assured they would have control over their own militias, the required three-fourths of the states ratified 10 of the amendments in what we now know as the Bill of Rights.

Many books on the Second Amendment are designed to direct you to one conclusion or another about the meaning of the Second Amendment and the need for guns. If you are looking for informative overviews with various narratives, I recommend reading Michael Waldman's *The Second Amendment: A Biography,* Adam Winkler's *Gunfight*, and Stephen P. Halbrook's *The Founders' Second Amendment: Origins of the Right to Bear Arms*. I'd also recommend selected portions from one of my favorite books, Jill Lepore's *These Truths, History of the United States.*

Whatever is debated today, recognize that the individual right to bear arms was not a specific item debated and discussed by our founders. People who could afford expensive, handmade guns had them, and in some states, militia duties were mandatory, as was having a gun to bring with you.

And what of our Founding Fathers' fear of a large standing army that could turn on its citizens?

The country's Continental forces gave way to the formalized US Army, Navy, and Marine Corps branches that fought in many wars in the succeeding years: the War of 1812, the Mexican American War, the Civil War, the Spanish-American War, and World War I. When each of those wars ended, most military personnel were decommissioned and sent home.

At the end of US involvement in World War II, for example, 12 million men and women wore a US uniform. Two years later, 10 million of them had been sent home. By 2022, the number of active-duty military had decreased to 1.4 million. With hundreds of millions of guns now in the hands of civilians, the founders' fear of strong-armed federal forces should have been a distant concern.

"I read that guns don't make homes safer; I don't believe that."

"Many studies validate this, even though people buy them for protection. An overwhelming number of guns are stolen from homes or used in domestic violence situations. The overwhelming reason most suicides happen at home is because that's where people have access to guns and millions of guns are unsecured. Every year this also results in a few hundred unintentional shootings by kids who find them."

Militia ... And More

But many still cling to Madison's notion that distrust of the government was their best position. Add to that another estimated 15 million preppers or doomsday preppers. These are Americans gathering survival essentials for their family or a group in anticipation of any number of potential catastrophic events that might disrupt or end modern civilization as we know it. Along with weapons, preppers stockpile food, water, and power backup systems among the top items on their to-get list. Survivalists, too, obtain weapons as part of their plan to go it on their own.

Some of those may know or be among the thousands, if not millions, on their own or part of a pro- or anti-government group, drill and equip themselves, believing they may be required to act to defend against tyranny or to be a force multiplier for law enforcement during an emergency.

The lines blur more when some foment violence, speak of distrusting the government, and have firearms in hand. Nowhere was this more evident than the uprisings against the government and assault on the US Capitol on January 6, 2021, as well as those convicted with the foiled kidnapping plots against the Michigan governor.

The Capitol assault resulted in charges filed against more than a thousand people, and jail sentences for scores of them, including charges for unlawfully carrying firearms onto the Capitol grounds. In Michigan, two were convicted, and another pled guilty to kidnapping conspiracy, while three others were convicted of gun charges and providing material support for terrorist acts as members of a paramilitary group. At one of the trials, it was revealed that then-Virginia Governor Ralph Northam was also a potential kidnapping target, perhaps because of the choice of gun-related laws he signed.

LOTS OF GUNS, FEW USED FOR VIOLENCE

Americans own an estimated 430 million guns. Of that number, only an infinitesimal number are involved in homicide deaths. For example, researchers looking at over 28 years of data found 118 shootings in which four or more people had been killed. Those involved a total of 228 weapons: 143 handguns, 55 rifles, and 30 shotguns.

How those weapons might be used to protect a person, his property, or in defense of his local or federal rights is interpreted in different ways by different people. Some might want to use their guns to change our democracy. Others believe they are the modern-day militia ready to fight tyranny and to protect our democracy. A 2013 Rasmussen Reports national telephone survey found that 65 percent of Americans believe that the purpose of their right to bear arms is still "to make sure that people are able to protect themselves from tyranny."

The challenge for this latter group of civilian gun owners is that federal and state laws do not grant civilians broad authority to fire on others. This leaves many legally able to carry a gun, but potentially liable for murder or other crimes if they use the gun.

GUNS OWNERSHIP WORLDWIDE

Dr. Adam Lankford, from the University of Alabama, has a thoughtful and well-researched world perspective on gun ownership and gun crimes. So, I went to Adam to discuss this international issue.

It is fair to say that we have A LOT of guns in the US. But I wanted to know how we compare to the rest of the world in gun availability and what their experiences are with terror in mass shootings and suicides.

Lankford set out a few years ago to answer that question, releasing his findings in 2016 that compare details on public mass shootings in 171 different countries. He knew that previous research consistently found that a high firearm ownership rate correlated with high homicide rates. One study of all 50 US states, he noted, found "strong correlations between local gun ownership rates and deaths from firearm-related homicides."

His research found that the US, which has less than five percent of the world's population, had 31 percent of global offenders. The remaining 69 percent is spread throughout the rest of the world. From 1966 to 2012, the US had five times the public mass shooters (90) as the next closest country. Those were the Philippines with 18, Russia with 15, Yemen with 11, and France at 10.

Lankford found that many of the nations that ranked highest in firearm ownership rates also ranked high in public mass shooters per capita. Other countries with high rates of firearms and public mass shootings include Yemen, Switzerland, Finland, and Serbia.

He did not find a similar association when it came to homicides and suicides. Countries that are considered very dangerous, such as Nigeria, Mexico, and Venezuela, he noted, had very few public mass shooting offenders.

Public mass shooters often spend time planning, many seek to commit suicide, and often shoot individuals who are strangers. This explains why homicide and suicide rates are similar in the US to other countries, even though public mass shootings flourish in the US and elsewhere.

"Perhaps the most obvious step the United States could take to reduce public mass shootings may also be the most politically challenging: reduce firearms availability," Lankford concluded. "It may take more cases of unambiguously successful gun control, such as Australia's, to begin to gradually change America's gun culture. Or it may take more scholarly research which provides empirical evidence of the link between firearms availability and public mass shootings and thus shows that policymakers and legislators may be able to directly influence the prevalence of these high-lethality crimes."

The most prophetic, or perhaps wistful, sentences in his study, however, are these:

"Ultimately, more cross-national studies of public mass shooters could help ensure that future strategies for prevention are based on reliable scientific evidence. Some countries and cultures are clearly safer than others; it would be a shame not to learn from them."

I know we disagree about many aspects in the gun debate, but can we agree to disagree about that and talk about some ways to better combat suicide in our community?

CHAPTER 5

Yesterday and Today's Gun Culture

A CULTURE BUILT WITH CHILD'S PLAY

That leads me to a common refrain I often hear that violent video games are to blame for mass shootings.

Violence has been woven into the fabric of American lives for decades. Video games are just the latest iteration. Generations alive today fought in wars and then came home to children playing on the floor with green plastic army men. Baby boomers remember cowboys chasing Indians with every "good" kid carrying a toy rifle, complete with gun belt and holster. They spent their days playing outside and their nights inside, watching justice served by the Lone Ranger or the Rifleman and by Marshal Matt Dillon.

Sunday night's Disney shows glorified Daniel Boone and Davy Crockett as well as their prowess with guns. The popularity of cap guns and Daisy Red Ryder BB guns waned only as paintball, Nerf guns, and home video game consoles became popular in the 1970s. Captain Kirk, James Bond, and Luke Skywalker replaced cowboys and other gun-carrying heroes, taking America's gun culture both internationally and into space on the big and little screens. Not much has changed.

Today, gun violence is wrapped up nicely under the categories of action movies and video games. Netflix rates the best gun movies, including gunslinging Westerns and epic shootouts. Modern warfare and urban violence both oblige.

Thirty years ago, dozens of psychologists from the American Psychological Association, gathering to look for answers to youth violence, noted the reality of violence in our culture.

"Our folk heroes and media images—from the cowboys of the old west to John Wayne, Clint Eastwood, and Arnold Schwarzenegger—often glorify interpersonal violence on an individual and personal level," they wrote in the Report of the APA Commission on Violence in Youth.

"Violent films are widely attended. American news media present image after image reflecting the violence in society, and in some cases may exploit or contribute to it. American football, one of the most violent of team sports, is an American creation. A plethora of guns and war toys are marketed and coveted and possessed by small children."

They didn't say it exactly this way, but after reading their notes, I think they concluded the culture we say we want is not the culture we embrace.

Hunting had been a sport of kings and a necessity for paupers for centuries, but violence-for-sport has become part of our modern culture. Therefore, it's too simple to point to video games as the problem when violence is everywhere around us. If you aren't watching it on your phone, home screen, or at the movies, you can head to Las Vegas and pay hundreds to have the "machine gun experience of your life" at one of the many entertainment venues.

This violence culture has fostered a sense of power and invincibility too, feeding into the credibility of the NRA-created talking point—the good guy with a gun.

CITY KID

Growing up in Michigan, I handled a gun only a few times and stayed home when classmates went north at the opening of hunting season. Instead, I concentrated on becoming a professional journalist, a bug I never shook after watching the Watergate hearings.

The day after I turned 18, I found work at the local daily newspaper, remaining there until I graduated from Michigan State University. A good newspaper job at the *Daily Herald* took me to Chicago, and before long, I had added a degree from DePaul University College of Law.

An offer to clerk for an appellate court justice led me to a prosecutor's job with the Cook County State's Attorney's office. Though I primarily worked drug cases, for a time I shared an office with a felony attorney who handled what we called the "dead baby cases." I admired her tenacity and told her I couldn't imagine not crying all the time if I worked through those horrific cases involving child victims.

When I joined the FBI, handling a gun became second nature. But I was happy to leave the drug cases behind and it came as somewhat of a relief to be working national security matters in their Milwaukee office, looking for terrorists, recruiting sources, and following the money trails. I felt the weight of the responsibility of counterintelligence investigations and the pressure when fate left me in charge as the supervisor of the Wisconsin terrorism response the morning of the September 11, 2001 attacks.

A promotion to the national counterintelligence division took me to Washington, D.C.; but, in the FBI, an agent works as assigned, and 15 years into my career, Sandy Hook happened, and my bosses sent me into the world of guns and mass shootings.

WHAT TO DO

When I was reassigned to the Biden effort after the Sandy Hook massacre, I became destined to learn about shootings across the country by their own short moniker: Clovis-Carver Library in New Mexico, Parkwest Medical Center in Tennessee, Kraft Foods and Minaret Temple in Pennsylvania, Accent Signs in Minnesota, McBride Lumber in North Carolina, Arapahoe High School in Colorado, and Café Racer in Washington.

From our first meeting, one or two on the White House team framed the entire issue as a gun debate. But we quickly realized that guns can quickly devolve into legislative and political debate that overshadows discussions about effective prevention programs and emergency preparedness. Even the terms firearms and guns are catch-all words for discussions about legislation, locks, availability, background checks, red flag laws, age restrictions, training, ammunition, magazine limits, and so much more.

The language of firearms can be tricky, particularly when we hear so many different terms thrown about in the news, on social media, and among our friends.

"I don't think there is any gun law or regulation that would work."

"I see it a little differently. Looking for one sweeping law to fix things isn't realistic since laws and regulation are complex. Some changes have helped, like banning minors and felons from owning guns. I'd like to work on fine-tuning and enforcing laws we have. For example, I'm frustrated the shrinking ATF's budget makes their enforcement efforts more challenging."

DEFINING MASS SHOOTINGS AND OTHER TERMS

Talking about active shooters means figuring out the difference between active shooter, mass killing, mass shootings, and other violence-related terms, such as serial killers and mass casualties. This confusion made it challenging to have conversations and prompted arguments about improperly used statistics, adding to the difficulty of interpreting numbers for research and training. As shootings have continued to rise and get increasing media coverage, the varied statistics have only complicated the discussions.

Many terms are used interchangeably, but have different and sometimes overlapping meanings. So, let's begin with some essential definitions.

An **active shooter** is an individual or individuals actively engaged in killing or attempting to kill people in a populated area. This definition is used by the FBI, Department of Homeland Security (DHS), Federal Emergency Management Agency (FEMA), and the rest of the federal government and, most notably, only involves firearms incidents. An earlier definition used by DHS included the words confined and crowded, but the FBI excluded confined because so many people misunderstood whether to include incidents occurring outside of a building. Yes, count them. A shooter running through a parking lot or running through a mall is still actively trying to kill people.

After Sandy Hook, Congress also chimed in, defining a **mass killing** as "three or more killings in a single incident" as defined by the Investigative Assistance for Violent Crimes Act of 2012, which was signed into law by US President Barack Obama a few weeks after the Sandy Hook killings. This statute also gives the FBI and DHS authority to assist in mass killing investigations at the request of local authorities where the incident occurs in "places of public use" or where attempted or actual mass killings occurred. Unfortunately, the statute fails to specify whether a deceased shooter should be included in the three. Law enforcement traditionally never includes the perpetrator in the death toll. But the statute calls for three killed, arguably allowing the shooter to be one of the three—perhaps something future legislators can modify. Though law enforcement never includes the killer, some researchers do, leading to further inconsistencies and confusion in data sets.

In much the same way, whether someone is killed or injured by an active shooter is not a determining factor in whether to count the incident. The shooter still causes the terror. Therefore, Oakland County Prosecutor Karen McDonald was able to obtain a guilty plea, including for murder and terrorism, from a high school shooter who killed four, injured seven, and terrorized about 180 survivors of the shooting at Oxford High School in Oxford, Michigan.

In April 2020, the DOJ took a big step forward to aid researchers by developing a singular definition for mass shootings, releasing the information in the *National Institute of Justice Journal* in an article entitled "Advancing Mass Shooting Research to Inform Practice." Authors Basia E. Lopez, Danielle M. Crimmins, and Paul A. Haskins concluded that inconsistent definitions and the lack of a comprehensive database were holding back meaningful research on how to end this type of violence.

Summarizing their findings, they wrote that "a common definition of mass shooting should be broad but not tied to any fixed minimum number of victims" and identified three elements of a mass shooting: (1) the discharge of a firearm in (2) "a single, continuous event, within an undefined timeframe," and (3) where there is "an evident premeditated intent to shoot to kill, regardless of the number of actual fatalities or injuries."

With this guidance, researchers are coalescing around this definition of **mass shooting:** "when an individual or individuals discharge a firearm, with premeditation, killing or attempting to kill multiple people in a single continuous event within an undefined timeframe."

An active shooter incident, therefore, is always a mass shooting incident, but not the other way around (e.g., mass shooter incidents that were not active shooter incidents include mass shootings discovered after they are completed, such as the July 2015 killing of nine in a church in Charleston, South Carolina, and the August 2016 killing of five family members in their home in Citronelle, Alabama). Active shooting numbers will be lower annually than other types of shooting, since we know most shootings and mass shootings occur in homes.

It is worth correcting a common misconception here—that the FBI uses the criterion of four or more victims to define the term mass shooting. The FBI has never used that number in mass shooting or active shooter research, though many researchers and writers have mistakenly indicated they do, including the DOJ in 2013.

Researchers may choose to disaggregate locations, offender characteristics, motivations, the number killed or injured, or the types of weapons used. The family members in Alabama were killed in the privacy of their home, and the church members' deaths were discovered well after the shooter had fled. So, you may see differences in the numbers media and researchers call out. Different numbers aren't wrong, they are just based on different criteria.

A 1998 federal statute, Investigation of Serial Killings, defines **serial killing** as three or more killed, but behavioral experts noted it was not so much a definition as it was a way to indicate when federal investigators could provide assistance. In its research on serial murder, the FBI chose to define the event as the unlawful killing of two or more victims by the same offender(s) in separate events.

Mass murder has no technical or statutory definition, and it and mass shootings are often used interchangeably by the media, writers, and researchers to describe the killing of multiple individuals, whether involving firearms or violence caused by knives, blunt instruments, vehicles, explosive devices, or other destructive means.

Mass casualty also is not defined, though it is the most expansive, counting the total killed or injured by any means during any human-made or natural disaster. In 2013, the research arm for the US Congress, Congressional Research Service (CRS), made up its own definition to identify what it called public mass shootings: "incidents occurring in relatively public places, involving four or more deaths—not including the shooter(s)—and gunmen who select victims somewhat indiscriminately." I don't know of any other researchers using this definition, but I am sure it helped inform Congress members.

Some researchers choose to use the term active attack when they want to track active shooter situations, but also include incidents where weapons in addition to firearms are used, such as knives and vehicles.

"With all of these guns around, I am afraid to let my kids go to their friend's house. I'm afraid a gun is tucked in a drawer or on a shelf and my kid will pick it up."

"That's scary. I'm sure you're not alone. We have guns in our house, but keep them locked up. Not everyone does that, but before I allow my own kids to go inside another child's house, I insist on a visit so I can meet the parents face-to-face. I straight out ask if there are any guns in the house because I think people should be frank about that. Would you be comfortable doing that? You can also make your house the house where kids come over."

HOW FAR APART ARE WE?

As I was exploring the nuances of the Second Amendment with my Spring 2021 class at DePaul University College of Law, the country was reeling with uncertainties from a nation-engulfing pandemic and election season.

Record gun sales reflected the fragility accompanying the pandemic as buyers said they needed to defend themselves during uncertain times. Relegated to the back of our minds were not-so-distant memories of 17 murdered and 17 injured at Marjory Stoneman Douglas High School and the scores of shootings that had followed.

"Gun debates aren't just about whether we should have guns or not," I told the class the first day. "To be good lawyers, you must understand not just why you do or don't want people to have guns, you must understand the history and laws surrounding the Second Amendment, cultural and political opinions, and how to bring someone over to your side of the issue."

It was my law students who unwittingly convinced me it was possible to add more to their education. The class makeup swung like a pendulum, from students believing every gun should be confiscated to those insisting the government has no authority to regulate gun ownership at all. Added to the mix was one particularly bright student from Canada who seemed gob smacked by America's gun obsession.

I had told them, to better understand today's gun debate, our path must take us through the various influences, including movies and television, rural and urban interests, the NRA, the complexities of quantifying any real numbers, and the role played by the US Supreme Court and Congress.

As our class progressed through the summer, students defended positions, often brilliantly and without vitriol. They represented imaginary clients' interests when I made them argue positions about which they did not agree. Many said they had started the class with a limited understanding of issues about which they had already formed opinions, such as an assault rifle ban. We talked about the unlikelihood of ever lifting all restrictions on gun ownership and debated the slew of laws passed or under consideration in various states, including mandatory registration, restrictions on gun sales and on the types of guns sold, as well as laws that would make it easier to take guns out of the hands of people who might be a danger to themselves or others.

They began to appreciate how much they had never been taught, and how divergent opinions were in the US.

Andrew Betts, who produces a news program for the website AR15.com, told me individuals should be able to carry any gun that a government person can carry, to keep the government in check. "Any weapon that is too dangerous to entrust to the people is far too dangerous to entrust to the government," he said, not explaining how an expansion of weapons of war available to civilians would work.

Betts speaks for many when he identifies his top two priorities: lifting the ban on fully automatic weapons and granting the right to all to carry a concealed weapon without a permit. Betts is very involved in the world of firearms products, laws, and policies. He speaks for some who dislike most or all gun regulations and oppose all permit and licensing fees, as well as purchase limitations and controls. Keeping guns from the hands of troubled people should not impact any of his rights with regard to firearms.

Equally troubling, he said, is the unwillingness of the ATF to prosecute straw purchasers or file other criminal charges against felons attempting to buy guns.

The deaths and turmoil caused by mass killings are big issues to tackle, Betts agreed, but laws and rules won't guarantee an end to the violence and human suffering. Instead, he said, collective efforts should focus on mandatory gun safety training in schools, mental health support, and other ways to ferret out those in trouble.

Not everyone agrees with Betts.

Joshua Friedlein, who was caught up in the 2015 Umpqua Community College shooting that left nine dead and eight others wounded, was in class elsewhere on campus in Roseburg, Oregon, when the lockdown order came in. His now-wife was in a building near where the shooting occurred. It was three hours "waiting to die," he told me. "Personal rights stop when you infringe on another and cause harm."

This is a rights/responsibilities conversation it is valuable to have briefly. It's a fair argument to say that the right to have a gun comes with responsibilities. Just like the right to have a driver's license comes with the responsibility to drive safely and not harm others.

Betts understands the responsibilities of gun ownership, as do all the gun owners I hang out with.

I heard one gun advocate say that the Constitution doesn't mention driver's licenses, so that's not a fair comparison. Legal scholars would counter that the Constitution has no words indicating farmers and business people have a right to carry a gun and yet here we are. So, arguing constitutional language is a non-starter. The Supreme Court and lower courts are making those calls. One consideration is how we can do a better job with the responsibilities that come with gun ownership. The US Supreme Court and other courts consistenly rule that gun rights are not absolute.

Friedlein had been homeschooled, and his father, a professional forester, and his grandfather had taught him to shoot in the small timber town where he'd grown up. They lived in a "red area," he said, referring to the Republican strength in Roseburg, where residents quickly stepped up to the cameras after the shooting to say they supported gun rights.

But the shooting changed Friedlein. He has joined the ranks as a Survivor Fellow with Everytown for Gun Safety and now supports universal background checks, red flag laws, and a ban on assault-style weapons.

No matter if you are on the "take all the guns away" side or "don't touch my guns" side, everyone can benefit from a better understanding of the nuances of firearms matters.

> **I know we disagree about whether people should be able to own guns, but can we agree to disagree about that and then talk about practical solutions to teach gun safety to those around them? We all want safer communities.**

Federal Legislation Over the Decades

TWO CENTURIES OF SILENCE

After the Bill of Rights was ratified, including its Second Amendment, the laws and attitudes about federal gun rights remained primarily static in the US. Any discussions of the limitations or rights of the Second Amendment simply didn't happen for much of the nation's first two hundred years.

Until 1986, the Second Amendment was known as the "lost amendment" because it was so rarely litigated or discussed, and this resulted in little guidance for lawyers and those looking to draft new legislation. But then, a handful of pivotal events throughout the 20th century set the wheels in motion to change the federal firearms landscape and give us the federal gun legislation and US Supreme Court decisions we live by today.

THE 1920S

The effects of the **Volstead Act**, the law enacting the Eighteenth Amendment, which ushered in the Prohibition era, also ushered in the gangster era.

The 1920s produced two significant federal firearms laws at a time when a small and outgunned federal law enforcement cadre faced weapons-laden gangsters willing to go to war with them, as well as other violent mobsters carving out territorial control of big cities.

The result was the **National Firearms Act of 1934** that was passed to confront organized crime violence during the Prohibition era. The law placed control over machine guns, short-barrel rifles and shotguns, and other weapons in the hands of what is now the ATF.

Quickly challenged, the US Supreme Court in *United States v. Miller* upheld the statute, with Justice James McReynolds writing,

> In the absence of any evidence tending to show that possession or use of a 'shotgun having a barrel of less than eighteen inches in length' at this time has some reasonable relationship to the preservation or efficiency of a well-regulated militia, we cannot say that the Second Amendment guarantees the right to keep and bear such an instrument.
>
> Certainly, it is not within judicial notice that this weapon is any part of the ordinary military equipment, or that its use could contribute to the common defense.

In short order, the **Federal Firearms Act of 1938** (FFA) established licensing for firearms sellers and prohibited gun sales to convicted felons and other prohibited individuals. This act was repealed by necessity when the **Gun Control Act of 1968** was passed and the provisions were incorporated into it, along with the FFA requirement in place today that requires sellers of firearms, FFLs, to be licensed.

THE 1960S

The period of civil rights and counterprotests and the rise of the Black Panther Party imposed tremendous pressure on legislators to re-evaluate firearms laws. Accompanying these events was the Supreme Court decision, *Brown v. Board of Education*, that found legislated racial segregation of public schools to be unconstitutional.

The 1960s brought additional opportunities for those seeking to tighten gun control after the assassinations of four men, two Black and two White.

The killer of President John F. Kennedy in Dallas in 1963 had bought his gun after clipping a coupon from a classified ad in the back of the NRA's magazine, *American Rifleman*. The rifle, scope-mounted, was shipped directly to a pawnshop in Texas, where he produced a $21.45 money order, and the gun was handed over to him.

Malcolm X, a human rights activist and Nation of Islam minister, spoke candidly about the double standard applied to gun ownership and the use of guns by Blacks versus Whites. At the same time, formative members of the Black Panther Party encouraged Blacks to use their legal right to openly carry guns to protect themselves and others, and they demonstrated their beliefs by patrolling the streets of Oakland, California, with shotguns and handguns.

This is a good place to pause and note that race considerations should be intertwined in a discussion of gun violence both because of the disparate impact gun violence has on those in the Black and Hispanic communities, and because for centuries laws, promulgated primarily by White state and local officials, operated differently for the races.

Blacks were prohibited from owning guns for nearly a century, and some of the actions of the Black Panther movement of the 1960s highlighted the widespread frustration engendered by a system that allowed Whites to openly carry while Blacks could not.

In the 1960s, when the Black Panthers exercised rights afforded them by open-carry gun laws to provide security for others, the swift legislative changes detailed below tightened the right to carry in a vivid demonstration of double standards based on race. Decades later, the Black Lives Matter movement, the protests and riots in the summer and fall of 2020 after the death of George Floyd, and ongoing race-focused struggles exemplify how complex these issues can be.

Fifteen months after President Kennedy's assassination, Malcolm X was assassinated.

Black Panther leaders marched to the California State Capitol in 1967 and read an open letter to then-Governor Ronald Reagan, stating, in part, "Black people have begged, prayed, petitioned, demonstrated, and everything else to get the racist power structure of America to right the wrongs which have historically been perpetuated against Black people. The time has come for Black people to arm themselves against this terror before it is too late."

The march prompted the swift passage of California's still intact **Mulford Act**, banning the carrying of weapons in the open. With the backing of other Republicans and the NRA, Reagan quickly signed the law, saying, "There's no reason why on the street today a citizen should be carrying loaded weapons." The act, he said, "would work no hardship on the honest citizen."

When the Reverend Martin Luther King, and presidential candidate, Senator Robert F. Kennedy, were assassinated, the Gun Control Act of 1968 was passed. The law banned mail-order sales, restricted certain high-risk people from purchasing guns, and prohibited the importation of military surplus firearms.

Both major political parties supported stricter gun laws, and the ban on mail-order sales of rifles, in particular. In 1968, the Republican Party platform called for the "enactment of legislation to control indiscriminate availability of firearms."

Testifying to Congress supporting the passage of the Gun Control Act, the NRA's Franklin Orth said some elements of the legislation "appear unduly restrictive and unjustified in their application to law-abiding citizens, but the measure as a whole appears to be one that the sportsman of America can live with." His comments were memorialized in The American Presidency Project, released by the University of California, Santa Barbara.

"That experiment by the Founding Fathers didn't work, so we need to repeal it."

"Many other countries allow citizens to own guns without having a Second Amendment, so I'm not sure that this is the quick solution to gun violence you are looking for. This is a democracy and right now the Constitution and the laws allow for gun ownership. Let's come up with something more immediate. I believe individual freedom to make our own choices is a very important concept for most Americans. I'd rather concentrate on insuring guns are safely handled and stored, and don't get into the hands of criminals or those who want to commit suicide."

THE 1970S

The publicly available record of the Republican Party platform of 1972 reflected a desire for gun control, calling to "intensify efforts to prevent criminal access to weapons." It provided for the "Enactment of legislation to control indiscriminate availability of firearms, safeguarding the right of responsible citizens to collect, own and use firearms for legitimate purposes, retaining primary responsibility at the state level, with such federal laws as necessary to better enable the states to meet their responsibilities."

By 1976, the political winds changed, and the gun debate would never again be the same.

In a widely covered coup, the NRA leadership was ousted at its 1977 annual convention and replaced by a slate of those who were more politically motivated. The NRA's motto, "Firearms Safety Education, Marksmanship Training, Shooting for Recreation," literally came down from the front of its building and, that same year, its newly opened, monolithic headquarters in Fairfax, Virginia, bore the words, "The Right of the People to Keep and Bear Arms Shall Not Be Infringed."

The Republican Party platform too changed in 1976, simply saying, "We support the right of citizens to keep and bear arms. We oppose federal registration of firearms."

THE 1980S AND 1990S

Another turn occurred after the assassination attempt on President Ronald Reagan in 1981, wounding him, his press secretary James Brady, Secret Service Agent Timothy McCarthy, and the District of Columbia Metropolitan Police Officer Thomas Delahanty. NRA money in a multitude of campaign buckets continued to make gun legislation an unlikely topic for legislation.

Yet, Congress passed the **1993 Brady Handgun Violence Prevention Act**, which amended the Gun Control Act. It required holders of FFLs to conduct a background check and established waiting periods on gun sales. The president's would-be assassin had purchased his small handgun at a pawnshop.

The **1994 Assault Weapons Ban** targeted the future manufacture, sale, and possession of combat-style assault weapons, as well as magazines carrying more than 10 rounds. Three former presidents—Gerald R. Ford, Jimmy Carter, and Ronald Reagan—sent a letter to all House members expressing their support for the measure before President Bill Clinton passed and signed it into law.

In their letter, widely reported in the press, the three former presidents said:

> This is a matter of vital importance to the public safety … Although assault weapons account for less than 1% of the guns in circulation, they account for nearly 10% of the guns traced to crime … While we recognize that assault-weapon legislation will not stop all assault-weapon crime, statistics prove that we can dry up the supply of these guns, making them less accessible to criminals. We urge you to listen to the American public and to the law enforcement community and support a ban on the further manufacture of these weapons.

Though the bill was signed into law, lobbying efforts successfully placed a 10-year sunset clause in the act and it died a natural death 10 years later. The law had no impact on firearms already owned.

With the exponential growth of NRA lobbying money filling campaign war chests, members of Congress passed no significant gun safety legislation in the succeeding 25 years. Though estimates exceeded $200 million in NRA spending since 1989, a mere $23 million was dedicated to the November 2020 federal races. As the NRA faced its own spending scandals and abuses by its executives, other advocacy lobbying organizations began to appear. For example, Gun Owners of America spent an estimated $880,000 on the 2020 election to flex its political muscle.

PROTECTING THE GUN MANUFACTURERS

In 2005, Congress passed the **Protection of Lawful Commerce in Arms Act**, which prevents firearms manufacturers and licensed dealers from being held liable for negligence when crimes are committed with their products. The NRA pushed for passage, arguing that the firearms manufacturers needed to be protected from the injuries suffered by the tobacco industry decades earlier.

In the 1950s and 1960s, the tobacco industry had used its lobbying efforts to neutralize federal and state clean indoor air legislation, minimize tax increases, and preserve the industry's freedom to advertise and sell tobacco. When scores of civil suits followed, the industry had to divert profits to pay legal fees. NRA lobbyists sought to keep their clients out of the courtroom, and the Protection of Lawful Commerce in Arms Act was the result.

Then, the **1996 Dickey Amendment** eliminated $2.6 million from the CDC's budget; the amount spent on firearms-related research the previous year. The amendment carried a stipulation that no funds be made available for injury prevention and control research or to advocate or promote gun control. Arkansas Republican Representative Jay Dickey had successfully attached the amendment to an omnibus spending bill, virtually ensuring its passage.

It was a "chilling message," Dickey later wrote in a 2012 *Washington Post* op-ed explaining his regret for bringing the amendment. He had been the "point man" for the NRA, he explained, and NRA executives were angry over their failure to suppress research published in the prestigious *New England Journal of Medicine*. That research found that residents with a gun in the home faced a 2.7-fold greater risk of homicide and a 4.8-fold greater risk of suicide.

In the editorial, Dickey conceded he pushed through the funding limits and, "[a]s a consequence, US scientists cannot answer the most basic question: What works to prevent firearms injuries? We don't know whether having more citizens carry guns would decrease or increase firearm deaths; or whether firearm registration and licensing would make inner-city residents safer or expose them to greater harm."

A total ban on research has been somewhat lifted by a reinterpretation of the Dickey amendment, but the damage was done with two decades of missed opportunity to fund gun control or gun safety measure programs and training.

When pressure subsided, a California study published in 2021 in the same publication, the *New England Journal of Medicine*, reported that in an examination of more than 25 million gun owners, men who owned handguns were almost eight times more likely to die of suicide. For women who owned handguns, that likelihood increased to 35 times.

"I don't lock my gun up because I need to be able to get to it fast."

"I get that. Actually, though, that's pretty dangerous because kids are pretty crafty and have been known to find them even if you think they are hidden. I can't imagine how I would feel if a kid found my gun and accidentally killed himself or someone else. In my home, we keep the guns locked up and teach gun safety. If you want, I could show you how quickly I can access the gun safe I own. There are gun safes that have quick access and can be hidden around the home too."

THE 2000S

No significant federal firearms-related laws were passed for the next 20 years. School shootings began to take center stage in the national debate on guns and violence. Beginning with the 1999 shooting at Columbine High School, news writers became somewhat obsessed with three factors at every major shooting story: did it happen at a school, what kind of gun was used, and was it legally purchased?

School shootings, in particular, mess with our psyche. We lived through shootings at Virginia Tech in 2007, Sandy Hook Elementary School in 2012, Marjory Stoneman Douglas High School in 2018, Oxford High School in 2021, Robb Elementary School in 2022, and Michigan State University and Covenant School in Nashville in 2023.

The deadliest shootings involved the use of semi-automatic or assault-style firearms and high-capacity magazines. These shootings ended multiple lives in seconds, sending an unimaginable shock through the affected communities. The Las Vegas shooter fired more than 1,000 rounds. The shooter at Pulse nightclub fired 211 rounds. The Covenant School shooter fired 152 rounds in 16 minutes. The Sandy Hook shooter fired 155 rounds in seven and a half minutes.

In any given year, more than 40 percent of US households report ownership of one or more guns, including an estimated 20 million semi-automatic rifles. Most households acknowledge they have had at least one unsecured gun at their house. Add those details with this fact. Nearly all the guns used in school shootings were legally purchased by someone, often the shooter.

The Sandy Hook shooter used a weapon his mother purchased legally for him, and they had gone shooting to get him out of the house. The Virginia Tech shooter purchased two handguns legally after instant background checks had been completed—one at a nearby pawnshop for $571 and the other online for $267.38. The Oxford High

School killer was given his gun as an early Christmas gift. He was 15 years old.

With the backdrop of a dramatic rise in active shooter situations from six-a-year on average to 60-a-year on average during a 22-year period, according to the FBI, the legislative winds of change shifted significantly after 19 children and two adults died at the elementary school in Uvalde, Texas.

THE BIDEN GUN LAW

When Joe Biden was sworn in as president on January 20, 2021, his ambitious agenda included a federal ban on the sale of assault weapons and a voluntary firearms buyback program. But 16 months later came the elementary school massacre in Uvalde, and the assault weapons and buyback ideas were shelved for lower hanging fruit.

"Their message to us was, 'Do something.' How many times did we hear that? 'Just do something. For God's sake, just do something.' Today we did," Biden said in a White House press event marking his signature to the nation's first substantive gun law in 30 years. That is the **Bipartisan Safer Communities Act** (Public Law No: 117-159) passed in the House 234-193 and the Senate 65-33.

The latest legislation demonstrates a more comprehensive view of tackling the rising gun violence problem. The 2022 act zeros in on areas that policy experts see as potential ways to stave off future firearms violence. It cobbles together a package attractive enough to lure all the Democrats and enough reluctant Republicans with varying priorities. For example, some elected officials wanted more violence intervention, as well as school and county mental health services. Others wanted more aggressive prosecutions for gun traffickers and straw purchasers. Some sought increased grant money for states and counties to enhance existing successful programs. Still others sought to strengthen criminal laws and enhance school security.

The new law engages with all these constituent demands, though likely change might not be noticed by everyone day-to-day.

The bi-partisan law has some provisions that deal directly with firearms, but also a slew of other provisions, such as $3 billion to clear court backlogs and $15 billion for research grants. Grants will go to a variety of children and family mental health services. More creative potential efforts, for example, can be found in a provision that requires the Centers for Medicare & Medicaid Services (CMS) to provide technical assistance and issue guidance to states on ways to improve access to telehealth under Medicaid and the Children's Health Insurance Program (CHIP).

Requirements for firearms purchases will be more visible, even if a limited number of people will be impacted by the changes. The law establishes new criminal offenses for straw purchasers or traffickers of firearms and extends federal firearms-related purchase restrictions for five years to those convicted of domestic violence misdemeanors against their dating partners.

One provision puts the focus on young shooters, some who may want to emulate other shooters or try to make themselves famous. The law expands background checks for persons between the ages of 18 and 21 by requiring investigators to do a deeper dive and scour "additional record systems—state criminal history or juvenile justice repositories, state custodians of mental health records, and local law enforcement agencies—for possibly disqualifying juvenile records."

Currently, background checks must be completed in three days, or the person automatically is allowed the purchase. These checks can be challenging to accomplish in the three days because there is no central repository for information that might be relied upon to determine if someone is prohibited from purchasing a gun as detailed in chapter three. States submit information into the FBI's NICS data base with varied thoroughness.

Convictions for incidents involving certain mental health matters, improper actions on military bases, and domestic violence, for example, may only exist in state mental health records or another federal or state criminal subject database. This requires NICS investigators to reach out to states where an individual has lived, hoping to capture all available relevant data.

If a potential purchaser is denied a gun purchase after an FFL runs their information through the NICS system, the results of that denial must be purged from the NICS system within 24 hours by federal law. Because of this, every search must start from the beginning and a determined buyer can simply go to another FFL the next day, and the next day and the next.

This three-day limit to run a background check is often referred to as the Charleston loophole, which is so named after nine Black people were killed at a prayer group in Charleston, South Carolina. The killer did not meet the criteria to purchase a gun, but his background check was not completed in three days, allowing the transfer of a gun to him.

After that tragedy, the FBI was asked how often that happened. They reported to Congress that between January and mid-November 2020, the FBI had flagged nearly 6,000 gun sales because a purchaser who could not legally possess a firearm was able to buy one because of the Charleston loophole—more than in any other entire calendar year.

The new law extends that background check time period from three to 10 days if cause exists for further investigation of anyone aged 18 to 21. Hopefully, someone is already finding a way to track whether this is effective because it has a 10-year sunset provision and will therefore no longer be enforceable in 2032 without reauthorization.

THE INTERNATIONAL IMPACT

In April 2020, a 51-year-old man dressed as a police officer and driving a fake police car shot and killed 22 people and set houses on fire in a 13-hour rampage in Nova Scotia. Three of the shooter's illegally owned weapons had been smuggled in from the United States. Catatonic over the idea of facing the same challenges the US now faces, the Canadian government announced sweeping changes to gun regulations.

It was one of several high-profile incidents that had occurred in the last decade.

Responding, Canadian legislators passed provisions in 2020 to ban 1,500 weapons and, prospectively, included language to prevent firearms manufacturers from skirting the ban by redesigning the gun. Currently, Canada is in the top ten countries globally in firearms ownership, suicide, and homicides. Gun lobbying groups and well-organized disinformation campaigns followed, putting some efforts on hold.

But it was not the first effort by Canada to deal with this burgeoning issue and it likely won't be the last.

Separately, the government announced an investment of $250 million through the Building Safer Communities Fund (BSCF) to help communities across the country prevent gun and gang violence by tackling its root causes, particularly for at-risk children. And its 2021 budget provided more than $312 million in new funding to increase firearms tracing capacity and implement stronger border control measures to fight gun smuggling and trafficking.

Canadian law enforcement agencies seized more than double the number of firearms at the border in 2021, compared to 2020, which is also the highest number of firearms seized in recent years.

The number of registered handguns in Canada increased by 71 percent between 2010 and 2020, reaching approximately 1.1 million, according to the Prime Minister's web page. Handguns were the most serious weapon present in most firearm-related violent crimes (59 percent) between 2009 and 2020. Canadian researchers have found victims of intimate partner violence are approximately five times more likely to be killed when a firearm is present in the home.

Canadian officials are moving with haste, specifically saying they don't want to be in the boat the US now finds itself.

> **I know we disagree about whether all semi-automatic rifles and handguns should be confiscated, but can we agree to disagree about that and then talk about teachers and others being able to carry a gun in school? We all want to solve gun violence and the more we talk about this complicated problem, the closer we get to solutions.**

CHAPTER 7

The Supreme Court and State Laws

THE SUPREME COURT

The ultimate guidance on individual gun rights granted by the Second Amendment is solidly enshrined in three landmark firearms cases, one decided in 2008, one in 2010, and the last one in the summer of 2022.

In the 2008 case, the Supreme Court decided a case called *District of Columbia v. Heller*. *Heller* involved a Washington, D.C., law that severely restricted the ability to own a handgun and required any gun to be registered and, if maintained in the home, to be either disassembled or protected with a trigger lock. The decision in *Heller*, written by Justice Antonin Scalia, did away with 100 years of limiting precedent to expressly find that the Second Amendment grants individuals a right to have a handgun in their home for self-defense.

The Court ruled that the Second Amendment was not just a right to be invoked for militia or military service, but also an individual right that could be used for "traditionally lawful purposes, such as self-defense within the home."

Led by those supporting a legal philosophy called originalism, the Court put its own meaning to the language. "We conclude that nothing in our precedents forecloses our adoption of the original understanding of the Second Amendment," the majority opinion stated.

Often quoted by gun advocates and referred to as justifying an absolute right to carry a gun, the case specifically says the opposite.

"Like most rights, the right secured by the Second Amendment is not unlimited," the Court wrote. "... nothing in our opinion should be taken to cast doubt on longstanding prohibitions on the possession of firearms by felons and the mentally ill, or laws forbidding the carrying of firearms in sensitive places such as schools and government buildings, or laws imposing conditions and qualifications on the commercial sale of arms."

The *Heller* decision listed what it might consider "presumptively lawful" regulations that could be passed by federal or state legislatures if they deemed the location to be "sensitive places."

"We also recognize another important limitation on the right to keep and carry arms," the *Heller* opinion went on to explain, citing *United States v. Miller*, 307 U.S. 174 (1939). "Miller said, as we have explained, that the sorts of weapons protected were those 'in common use at the time.' [citation omitted] We think that limitation is fairly supported by the historical tradition of prohibiting the carrying of 'dangerous and unusual weapons.'"

Shortly after, in 2010, in *McDonald v. Chicago*, the Court strengthened the *Heller* decision by saying that through the 14th Amendment, *Heller* applies in all states.

Then, in 2022, in the long-anticipated decision in *New York State Rifle & Pistol Association Inc. v. Bruen*, the US Supreme Court struck down a New York law exploring the right to carry a weapon in public places for self-defense.

The New York state law made it a crime to possess a firearm without a license, whether inside or outside the home. The law stated that any individual who wanted to carry a firearm outside their home was only allowed to do so if they obtained an unrestricted license to "have and carry" a concealed "pistol or revolver" and then only if they could prove that "proper cause exists" for doing so, according to the Court's opinion. The law also required gun permit applicants to show they are of good moral character.

An applicant could satisfy the "proper cause" requirement, the court noted, only if they could "demonstrate a special need for self-protection distinguishable from that of the general community."

The Court's ruling in the *New York Pistol* case retained the *Heller* standard that allows legislatures to prohibit firearms in "sensitive places." Though the *Heller* court shed some light on potentially sensitive places, the *New York Pistol* court was not explicit.

"In addition to polling places, the Court specifically named legislative bodies and courthouses," they posted on their website. "But the Court did not define sensitive places or address other places of mass congregation, such as protests and public transportation. Future lawsuits will probably have to find similarities between modern prohibitions and historically regulated 'sensitive spaces' to determine whether contemporary gun laws are constitutional."

Together, these three cases are fascinating and steeped in challenging interpretations of the Constitution that do not necessarily match what so many of us learned as lawyers in training.

Lawyers and other constitutional scholars recognized the expanse of the ruling immediately. The New York law at issue is almost superfluous.

Legal challenges going forward are likely to face the challenge of revisiting the entire history of laws, culture, and opinions dating back to when the US was a colony. This is because the Court itself said consideration for new legislation must reflect the laws and views held at that time.

Shortly after the Supreme Court's landmark decision in *New York Pistol*, the interpretations began when a lower federal court judge in New York imposed a temporary restraining order that blocked New

York laws banning guns in many public places, including campgrounds, subways, and Times Square.

"I like Texas' new law eliminating licensing and training so now I can carry my handgun anywhere I want."

"I think that is sending us backwards. That's like allowing people to drive without any training, except this is allowing someone to carry a lethal weapon around in public. I don't think that makes us safer, do you?"

STATE LAWS

Though federal legislative changes are rare and federal court rulings are less frequent, states can change their laws and regulations quickly. States laws can better reflect the desires of the community. This impacts a community and the police, who must know and enforce the changes.

Every new state legislative session brings lobbyists looking for change, parents impacted by violence, and lobbying groups who find attempting change at the state level less daunting than at the federal level. State legislatures often move fast, reacting when a spectacular shooting occurs or when the right mixture of politicians is elected for a particular term.

In the 2018 legislative session, dozens of substantive changes were made to state gun laws. Connecticut, Vermont, and Maryland banned the possession of bump stocks, a device that allows a semi-automatic rifle to fire like an automatic rifle. Wyoming and Idaho codified stand your ground laws, allowing for a gun owner to be exempt from prosecution in some circumstances when he chooses not to retreat from a threat in a public place.

Wyoming dropped churches from its list of prohibited places to carry a gun. South Dakota passed a law allowing guns to be carried in non-public schools teaching kindergarten through 12th grade. West Virginia passed a law preventing property owners from being able to prohibit lawfully owed guns in vehicles parked on that owner's private parking lot or land.

State Supreme Courts also impacted local rules. The Michigan Supreme Court ruled that kindergarten through 12th grade schools may prohibit the open carrying of weapons on their campuses while a Delaware Supreme Court ruling struck down a ban on carrying guns in state parks and forests.

The details of gun laws may not be as important in some places. Montana residents, for example, have no restrictions on open or concealed carry for handguns even in restaurants that serve alcohol. No permits are required for the possession or sale of semi-automatic guns and high-capacity magazines. The ability to carry concealed without a permit has been outfitted with the appealing name of constitutional carry.

But in some states, expansive changes can take place seemingly overnight when legislature takes control. Virginia is perhaps the best recent example of this, a state where firearms use is the leading cause of death among children and teens. Six months after the 2019 Virginia electors turned the legislature into a momentary Democratic majority, then-Governor Ralph Northam signed seven new laws further defining gun control access in Virginia.

Virginia has had its share of infamous gun tragedies. In 2019, a disgruntled municipal worker in Virginia Beach killed 12 people. In 2017, six people were injured, including then-US House Republican

Majority Whip Steve Scalise, when a shooter opened fire at a baseball field in Alexandria where members of Congress were practicing for their annual charity fundraiser. In 2015, a news reporter and a photojournalist in Roanoke were shot and killed by a recently fired employee during a live television broadcast. In 2010, two police officers were injured during a shootout at the busy train platform outside a security checkpoint at the Pentagon in Arlington County. In 2007, the Virginia Tech shooter killed 32 people. In 2006, an 18-year-old shooter ambushed two Fairfax County police officers during a shift change just a mile from my house.

Northam, who is a pediatric neurologist and was a medic in the US Army during Operation Desert Storm, said the 2019 legislative efforts stopped short of his desire to also enact some sort of assault weapons ban. "We don't need those weapons on the street," he told Courthouse News. "If anybody thinks they are needed, I'd ask them to go into a mass casualty tent to get a glimpse of what they do to human beings."

The new laws reflect concerns like those expressed by Vijay Katkuri. Katkuri told the *New York Times* he voted Democratic in the 2018 midterm election because of "guns." He said, "That is the most pressing issue for me. There are lots of other issues, but you can only fix them if you are alive."

Once the capital of the Confederacy, and the current home of the NRA, Virginia has long had some of the country's most lax gun laws. The legislature's approach was sweeping. A portent of changes to come in some other states, the boutique package surgically closes disparate loopholes in laws involving not only gun sales but also gun safety for children and people in crisis. Signed into law in 2020, were the following:

- A law requiring gun owners to report their lost or stolen firearms to law enforcement within 48 hours or face a civil penalty.
- A law making it a Class 1 misdemeanor (an increase from Class 3) when the reckless act of leaving a firearm unsecured allows a minor under the age of 14 to access a firearm.
- A law requiring persons to sell or surrender to law enforcement, or a person authorized to have a firearm, all firearms within 24 hours of being served notice of a domestic violence restraining order (known as a permanent protective order) with a maximum duration of two years.
- A law expanding the authority of local communities to ban firearms in "sensitive areas."
- A law establishing judicial authority to issue Extreme Risk Protective Orders, those *red flag* laws, which create a legal mechanism for law enforcement and the courts to temporarily separate a person from their firearms with a determination they represent a danger to themselves or others.
- A law limiting handgun purchases to one a month for nearly everyone; a law passed to help curtail stockpiling of firearms as well as firearms trafficking.
- A law requiring criminal background checks for nearly all gun sales, with exceptions for family and a few other unique relationships. This closes what is commonly mis-characterized as the gun show loophole, though this is law is not about gun shows but private gun sales.

In 2021, legislators passed another set of measures, including a three-year ban on firearm possession for some people convicted of assaulting a family member. Research shows a strong correlation between mass shooters and domestic abuse, especially against women.

Virginia governors can only serve one term, however, and the Democrats narrowly lost the top spot with the swearing in of Republican Governor Glenn Youngkin in January 2022. The new governor quickly vowed to try to dismantle the gun laws if his Republican party could wrestle control of the state senate, since it already controlled the lower house.

Critics of the governor noted that Virginia persists in being the site of some of the most spectacular mass shootings. Two days before Thanksgiving in 2022, a disgruntled manager at a Walmart in Chesapeake pulled out a handgun at a staff meeting and killed five coworkers and a 16-year-old boy before killing himself. He had purchased the handgun just hours before. Earlier in the month, a University of Virginia student allegedly shot three football players on a team bus.

"The Supreme Court upheld the Second Amendment last year, so I don't think there is any point in talking about regulating guns."

"If you mean the New York case, the Bruen decision, I think you are misunderstanding the role of the Supreme Court. Just like the Court's decision in Heller in 2008, the justices were asked very narrow questions to evaluate whether a given state law was Constitutional. In both cases, the written opinions are very interesting reads about when and how firearms should be controlled. The Bruen case, for example, only dealt with a law on an individual's right to carry a handgun outside their home."

The NRA balked when Virginia passed its package of statutes, and it announced it would move from Virginia. But it did not.

Not all states are moving in the direction of Virginia, although political candidates continue to receive the support and financial backing from advocate groups such as the Coalition to Stop Gun Violence, the Brady Campaign to Prevent Gun Violence, and Everytown for Gun Safety. Everytown includes both Moms Demand Action for Gun Sense in America and Mayors Against Illegal Guns, largely funded by former New York City Mayor Michael Bloomberg.

Some states are arming teachers. In recent years, Texas and Georgia have legalized the carrying of a concealed handgun at all institutions of higher education—with Georgia also allowing knives, knuckles, bats, clubs, and nunchucks. The law stands even though gun owners and non-gun owners in campus communities largely believe that allowing concealed carry on a campus will harm the academic atmosphere and diminish a feeling of safety in contentious situations.

After the shooting in Parkland in 2018, Florida legislators approved an Extreme Risk Protection Order statute (ERPO), raised the minimum age to purchase a long gun to 21, enacted a three-day waiting period on purchases from dealers, and closed the Charleston loophole for Florida gun purchasers by requiring a background to be completed no matter how long it takes. Florida legislators also authorized adding more people with guns inside school through a program called the Guardian Program, which will include the arming of some teachers.

No matter the current state legislation and when it was signed into law, the *Bruen* decision is an invitation to challenge it. Winkler, who wrote the book *Gunfight* mentioned earlier, told the *Daily Press* in Newport News, Virginia that: "Bruen basically supercharged Second Amendment litigation." It makes it likely, he said, that "just about any gun law on the books (is) going to be challenged on the basis that there were not similar laws in the 1700s and 1800s."

> **I know we disagree about what guns people should be able to own, but can we agree to disagree about that and then talk about our mutual fear of shootings in schools or in the public, and some of the ways we might take away that fear, for our kids too, if we are better informed and prepared?**

CHAPTER 8

Not Gonna Happen, Might Happen

When gun violence enters public discussion, waves of potential solutions are free flowing. Some are new ideas. Some have been around for a long time. Whoever has the loudest microphone may pitch their idea as if it is a panacea.

But my years of working in this area have taught me that no single law, policy, or change in society will stop gun violence on its own. We must keep our focus on multiple efforts. This is not just one idea, but the many that can work together to reach our goal.

What ideas are the best to pursue? There are many out there. I categorize them in two buckets: not gonna happen and might happen.

The first bucket might have good or interesting ideas, but some aren't practical or likely ever possible. Many in the second bucket of might-happen ideas involve uphill climbs. But collectively I find them promising in the fight to reduce gun violence.

Each takes a willingness to talk about our situation honestly and together step into the fray to do the work to turn the ideas into reality. There are more ideas in the might-happen bucket, too many to write about. But the ones I note will take tremendous political will.

Many more might-happen options are being tested in pockets at the state and local level.

State laws may prove to be good incubators for ideas that could be extended nationwide. Research will identify the successes of state laws, including one-gun-a-month purchase limits, waiting periods for cash to carry, red flag laws, and limitations on the purchase of ammunition and high-capacity magazines.

Here are the most talked about ideas and where and why they are on my list.

NOT GONNA HAPPEN

To be clear, I'm not saying any idea to stem gun violence is meritless or may never come to pass. Many I list are intriguing but would require a seismic change in our culture and our laws. We've accomplished seismic change before. I am reminded of the abolition of slavery, protection of voting rights for all sexes, the lowering of the voting age to 18, and the establishment of Social Security, Medicaid, and Medicare.

Reducing gun violence will take ideas built for seismic change, but those ideas may not yet be ripe for success. Individuals strongly dedicated to these ideas can and should continue to pursue policies, procedures, and political changes they believe in. But in the short term, the concern is that they take up a lot of oxygen when the rest of us could focus that breath on actions more likely to be executed now in our own homes and neighborhoods.

Repeal of the Second Amendment

Let me explain why the repeal of the Second Amendment is at the top of my *not-gonna-happen* list. To repeal an Amendment, another amendment must be proposed and signed into law, a tremendous undertaking. This has happened only once in our history when the 18th Amendment (Prohibition) was repealed by the 21st Amendment.

Repealing the Second Amendment is an idea that has been bandied about for years. In an op-ed piece in the *New York Times* in 2018, US Supreme Court Justice John Paul Stevens recommended repealing the Second Amendment. He favored an alternative amendment that clarified the firearms rights ownership for members of state militias. At the time, the Senate historian estimated that about 11,700 amendments had been proposed and only the language of the 21st Amendment had been successfully approved.

Only the United States, Mexico, and Guatemala have Second Amendment-style language in their constitutions. Our Constitution, in Article V, requires that to make a change, an amendment must be proposed by two-thirds of the House and Senate, or by a constitutional convention called for by two-thirds of the state legislatures. And in the end, it is up to the states to approve any new amendment, with three-quarters of the states required to vote in favor of ratification.

The 18th Amendment and its ratification took about 14 months, prohibiting nearly every aspect of alcohol activity except the actual drinking of alcohol. It wasn't until Franklin Delano Roosevelt included a repeal proposal on the platform for his 1932 presidential bid that a repeal gained the right traction. The 21st Amendment was proposed in Congress in February 1933, and the ratification completed in December of that year.

Since then, Congress has passed a few other proposed amendments, but the states have failed in the ratification stage.

For example, an Equal Rights Amendment (ERA) was initially proposed in Congress in 1923 to secure full equality for women, seeking to end the legal distinctions between men and women in terms of divorce, property, employment, and other matters. Congress finally accepted language and passed the ERA 50 years later in 1972. The five-year time period for ratification was extended another three years and still only 35 of the necessary 38 states ratified, dooming it to failure.

The language of the proposed Equal Rights Amendment was: "Equality of rights under the law shall not be denied or abridged by the United States or by any state on account of sex."

To date, this simple language amendment has not been ratified by the states of Utah, Arizona, Oklahoma, Missouri, Louisiana, Arkansas, Georgia, Alabama, Mississippi, North Carolina, South Carolina, and Florida.

If through the decades this simple language could not meet political agreement for an amendment, who can truly believe our panacea for ending gun violence is to adopt another amendment to repeal the Second Amendment?

"I think we should repeal the Second Amendment."

"That's cool. I'm not in that camp, but I respect you are. I believe the Second Amendment is there to protect citizens from abuse by the government and from other threats to our physical safety. No one is forced to own a gun. At the same time, no one should be prevented from owning a gun unless there is a good reason, so maybe we need to work better on those reasons."

Mandatory Confiscation, Buy Back of All Guns, or the Buy Back of Semi-Automatic Pistols and Rifles

A mandatory gun buyback is a common volley in gun violence discussions. It seems reasonable to say, "Hey, we'll pay you to give up your guns."

Here are just two of the reasons why this is on my not-gonna-happen list.

First, recall that the number one reason people say they buy a gun is for protection. At any given time, around 30 percent or 40 percent of American households have guns. Even though every law enforcement officer I know says they would like to see fewer guns in circulation, gun owners counter by pointing out that most of their guns remain at home. Every poll shows that gun owners overwhelmingly say it's a bridge too far to require them to sell their guns to the government. They will not support it politically. Remember, gun owners vote too.

Even if for some reason gun owners willingly sold their guns back for destruction, another factor that would impact even non-gun owners would likely put a break to the plans. That second reason is math.

Most discussion about buybacks begins with a reference to the successful 1990s mandatory buyback effort in Australia initiated after 35 people were killed and another 28 wounded during a massacre in Port Arthur. In one of the many actions that followed, Australia mandated the collection of privately owned semiautomatic guns and pump-action rifles.

In total, approximately 650,000 were bought back with $304 million dollars paid in compensation. At the time, Australia had an estimated three million firearms in private hands, so this involved about 21 percent of the guns in that country.

This is the math part. If there are about 425 million guns in the US and estimates put 20 percent of those in the category of semiautomatic handguns and rifles, that totals 85 million firearms. Australia paid approximately $468 per weapon confiscated. If the US Congress decided to muster a similar buyback program, it would need to budget about $40 billion for the payments, even if owners only received $468 for each one. **But if you read to the end of this book, you'll see why the cost isn't a factor when Americans demand a solution.**

To be clear, many local communities have launched buy back efforts through the years to reduce the guns locally, Philadelphia, Baltimore, Seattle, and Washington D.C., among them. These generally offer a nominal cash payment or gift cards when guns are turned in. Most communities have those guns destroyed, although I know a few who, astonishingly, resell them to help their budget.

Research establishes that some guns turned in were damaged, some were worth less than the offering, others were once owned by someone now deceased, and some were just sold because a gun owner wants the gun out of the house. Those are all good reasons, but it's worth noting here that anyone can voluntarily turn a gun in to law enforcement, no questions asked, and if you want to help end gun violence, the need for a $100 Walmart gift card should not be your motivating factor.

A national buyback could have been in our crystal ball many decades ago before gun manufacturers and the NRA made buying multiple guns so attractive. By sheer coincidence or divine intervention, one of the editors for this book was an Australian. She dropped a note in the manuscript to say there are plenty of firearms for ranchers, hunters, and sportspeople in Australia, but otherwise, there isn't much interest in gun ownership among the general population. Their culture does not cry out for it.

But for now, in the US, the lack of will to change our culture and undertake such an endeavor means a national buyback effort is on my not-gonna-happen list.

Establish a National Gun License for Gun Purchases

Easily compared to the need for a driver's license, many countries have a national requirement that potential firearms purchasers first be licensed to own a gun.

In countries that require licenses, applicants may have to be interviewed, provide character witnesses, and accept a waiting period for purchase. Some licensing requires the licensee to train first, prove they have a place to lock up guns, and pass mental health evaluations.

Allowing someone a license also creates a system that allows the government to invalidate a license if conduct warrants cancellation.

Most states have no permit requirements to own a shotgun or rifle. And about half of our states require someone to obtain a permit if they want to carry a handgun outside of their house.

Advocates for national gun licensing will continue to seek ways to license gun purchasers, perhaps starting with future purchasers. Many gun owners I know have come to support this idea after witnessing who has been allowed to buy a gun, particularly in the past decade.

But for the roughly 80 to 100 million adults who say they already own a gun, evaluating them and granting them licenses at the national level seems an uphill climb. Though a majority of those polled say they would like to see it happen, it would literally take an act of Congress and there does not seem to be a will to make it happen.

"I'm afraid to talk to my kid about guns. It scares me."

"It might help if you focused on discussing something besides gun violence. I grew up in a house with several guns. They were locked up in my parents' bedroom and we knew we were not allowed to go in there. Mostly, those guns were used for small game and deer hunting. When those seasons came around every fall, my dad would bring out a gun and do some target shooting to get ready to go hunting. I learned to think of the guns as tools that were used for a specific purpose."

Registering All Guns in the US

Developing a national register may be a laudable goal for those who see it potentially aiding the need to follow the movement of guns eventually used in a crime. Perhaps a registration list would aid in notifying buyers of manufacturer information and law enforcement would be more likely to know if a gun is associated with a person, car, or home with which they interact.

Advocates for this voice a variety of benefits. For example, advocates say registration could help identify homes where children live, and mandatory gun safety training can be offered.

Accomplishing this would be challenging. First, how can we track down the physical volume of guns likely spread throughout every nook and cranny of our more than 3.5 million square miles? This would be a monumental task. How would we capture the guns that are manufactured and modified in private homes? How would we track guns sold in private sales? Would we require registration of inoperable guns, guns passed along in inheritance, and firearms in antique collectors' hands?

Americans own an estimated 40 percent of the world's guns, though we have less than five percent or the world's population. This endeavor would likely require a new government component to simply manage the information on gun sales between all individuals. The ATF is notoriously underfunded and can't even digitize many of its records, a prohibition seemingly designed to simply make gun tracing more difficult.

Even if Congress was willing to fund a registration program, every person with firearms in their home would have to be willing to not only register their firearms by some means such as serial numbers and digital photos, but they would also be required to attach their name to that registry. This, by default, would result in a national registry of gun owners; something so many gun owners oppose. Many gun owners might be willing to register their firearms, but practically speaking, this is not gonna happen soon.

Counting on the Good Guys with Guns

I'm going to put this on the list of not gonna happen, because reality slaps the face of those who support this as the panacea. If more guns solved the problem, we would have the safest country in the world.

The truth is that only a handful of incidents a year result in a true good guy with a gun scenario. When school shootings and other mass killings began to increase dramatically in the past 15 years, the NRA, politicians, and pundits—those opposing any firearms regulations—popularized this mantra with no data to support it: "The only thing stopping a bad guy with a gun is a good guy with a gun." It's a nice sentiment, or at least a catchy phrase, but research now tells us it is not founded and particularly when the most violent and public shootings happen.

The FBI documented only four instances where an armed civilian killed an active shooter when evaluating 345 active shooter incidents between 2000 and 2019. They found another six where gunfire was exchanged for some period, but no bullets hit their mark. In one additional situation, an armed civilian who pursued a shooter into a store was shot and killed before he could fire his gun. That same FBI research found 33 active shooter incidents where unarmed civilians successfully stopped a shooter.

Responding to a shooting is stressful for even highly trained law enforcement. Officers can accidentally discharge their firearm and miss their targets, sending bullets to unforeseen, innocent people standing near or behind their target.

Another inherent flaw in the overall "good guy with a gun" theory is an assumption that a person who owns a gun would have it accessible, have it loaded, be particularly proficient in hitting their intended target, and not get killed by another shooter or a law enforcement officer who understandably might believe they are the aggressor.

As a trained law enforcement officer, I cannot overstress that weapons proficiency is a continuing, lifelong effort and anyone discharging a firearm in public must appreciate the stress, discipline, and responsibility it involves. It's just not realistic to pin hopes on someone nearby with a gun.

Civilians without consistent repetitive training are less likely to have the muscle memory to draw and fire accurately under pressure. Shooters must be in the right place, with their equipment read, at the right time to be able to protect themselves and still end the threat. Shooting incidents in public are replete with situations where even trained law enforcement offers were unable to intercede successfully to prevent a loss of life.

Twenty years of data disproves the theory that putting guns in the hands of civilians will have a positive impact on reducing targeted violence.

Some argue that carrying is necessary, particularly in states with zones prohibiting firearms. But shootings do not impact states based on politics. The highest number of active shooter incidents tracked by the FBI have occurred in California, Florida, Texas, and Pennsylvania—the most populated states.

This applies to gun-free school zones too, although more schools than ever are arming teachers. On my last check, 28 states had laws allowing school districts to arm teachers and staff. A few states even pay to train them and provide the guns. This includes Alabama, Arkansas, Colorado, Florida, Georgia, Hawaii, Idaho, Indiana, Iowa, Kansas, Massachusetts, Michigan, Minnesota, Mississippi, Missouri, Montana, New Hampshire, New Jersey, North Dakota, Ohio, Oklahoma, Oregon, South Dakota, Tennessee, Texas, Utah, Washington, and Wyoming.

Debates rage over whether a teacher would be able to shoot one of their own students pointing a gun at them or whether a teacher might shoot a student in the heat of an argument.

Scores of incidents have been documented where school officials have left guns in bathrooms, in desks, and elsewhere. In Idaho, a college chemistry professor accidentally shot himself in the foot during a class just months after lawmakers there passed a law allowing firearms on state campuses. At the time, a national survey of more than 900 college presidents found that 95 percent opposed permitting concealed weapons on campuses. National Education Association (NEA) members and other teacher and school administrator associations also released formal statements opposing arming teachers.

After US Education Secretary Betsy DeVos sought in 2018 to use federal Student Support and Academic Enrichment grants to allow the purchase of guns and to train teachers, immediate opposition was voiced by the NEA, the American Federation of Teachers, the National Association of School Psychologists, the National Association of Secondary School Principals, and the National Association of Elementary School Principals.

The American Bar Association agreed: "There are many known, evidence-based means to address the complex issue of school shootings. Arming teachers is not one of them."

Arming teachers is truly a local decision and may depend on variables, such as the distance between the school and first responders. But schools that choose to arm teachers should do so in a thoughtful and comprehensive fashion, including adding gun safety to their kindergarten through 12th grade curriculum. This would prepare them for the inevitable situation where an exposed gun may be within reach of a child. The state of Michigan has had this option on the books for 10 years with few takers.

One final fact about data. Trained law enforcement officers have neutralized shooters as have unarmed civilians. No research to date shows good guy teachers with guns have made schools safer. We might have that data someday, but we don't today.

"My sister wants to buy a gun for protection, but I told her she's nuts."

"Some people think a gun is a great equalizer in a confrontation, and I try to respect that, but it isn't always that simple. Studies show homes with guns have higher incidents of firearms deaths."

"I think it will be more dangerous and won't keep her safe."

"Have you thought about asking her how she thinks it will make her safer? You have a right to be concerned because carrying a gun is an enormous responsibility. You might ask her how she'll keep it secure, how much practice she'll have, and where she will carry it. I know that carrying a gun can often be cumbersome and not allowed in areas like parks, schools, and buildings, prompting people to leave their guns under car seats and in bags where they can be stolen. That's where most guns are stolen from."

"She's going to get it, no matter what I say."

"You might take the time to talk to her about it more and maybe you will feel better, no matter what she decides. Make sure you discuss with her whether you would allow the gun at a family gathering or in your home too, if that might be an issue."

CHAPTER 9

Might Happen

Before turning to some of the more promising or impactful ideas that might happen, I want to provide an opportunity for you to eavesdrop on a conversation I had with one of the many people dedicated to this mission who do not work withing government offices.

Looking back at successes that lifted us from the Depression, we sometimes forget about monumental public/private partnerships that help sustain us during some of our direst days. One such was the Reconstruction Finance Corporation (RFC) during the 1930s. The RFC's worked with the federal government to successfully channel private capital to preferred private efforts. Critics might say favoritism occurred, no doubt, but the RFC gave investors the confidence to believe they would benefit from spending at such a nervous time.

Today, most may be unaware of the many public/private efforts sinking hundreds of millions into the fight against this public health crisis. Among the leaders are Arnold Ventures, the RAND Corporation, John Hopkins Center for Gun Violence Prevention and Policy, the American College of Surgeons, and the National Collaborative on Gun Violence Research. Many, many other similar efforts are underway.

The names are similar, the goals nearly identical. They are pouring money into first-of-its-kind research, training, and policy recommendations as well as support to guide organizations that use government grant money.

Another tremendously ambitious and successful effort is The Institute for Firearms Injury Prevention based at the University of Michigan, and their cooperative effort with the National Center for

School Safety. I'm humbled to say I've been tapped often as an expert by the Center.

I've had many conversations about mass shootings, firearms injury prevention, and ways to end gun violence with the Institute's co-director, Marc Zimmerman.

He has dedicated his entire professional academic and research career to strengthen individuals and communities so they can build resilience. He likens it to nurturing a healthy garden instead of waiting for trouble and then being forced to weed and use pesticides.

He believes the Institute's firearm research and potential changes to laws and policies can help guide the US into the cultural shifts needed to reduce firearms violence. Not too many years ago, he noted, car crashes were the number one cause of death in America. In his own words:

> We invested literally billions of dollars over a 60-year period. And you probably remember when we first got seat belts. We've transformed society. Everybody puts one on. It's become part of our culture. We've actually changed culture and we reduced the number of deaths by car crashes by 80 or 90 percent.
>
> We've done that with engineering solutions, behavioral solutions, policy solutions. Multiple solutions. Roads are safer, tires are better. Cars have airbags. The seat belts are better. We have graduated licensure because we did studies that we found most people got in the car crashes from the ages of 17 to 21. We started developing policies and strategies for all of that.
>
> We have to do the same thing about firearms because in 2017 in the United States, the number of deaths by firearms

surpassed those by cars. And it has been, and has stayed, separate ever since. The lines are going in completely different directions. The car crash line was staying flat, and we had policies around and media campaigns about don't drink and drive, don't let your friends drink and drive, and distracted driving. We understood what was going on.

We need to do that kind of research so we can translate that into policies and program about firearms injury prevention. We're not—at least in the institute—were not talking about gun control. We're not talking about taking away people's gun. We're not going after the Second Amendment. We're about gun safety.

There's close to 400 million guns in private hands in the United States and that doesn't include police guns or any military guns. There are over one hundred million homes with a firearm in it. There are 40, getting closer to 50,000 deaths. Estimates for (firearms) injuries which we don't have good data on yet, unfortunately, is 60 to 100,000 people are injured by firearms. When you start doing the math, it's actually relatively small. 40,000 people in a country of 350 million. But it's not just one person. It's their siblings. It's their family. It's their extended family. It's their community.

I don't want to vilify gun owners, that's not the point. We could be safer, just like we could drive cars, and we've succeeded with all these solutions while people are driving faster and there's more people driving and more cars on the road. We've succeeded in doing that and we need to do the same thing here. We haven't done anything like this for firearms.

> We've can put people on the moon, and we can reduce crashes in cars. We have to be able to do better than we're doing now.

Ever the researcher, Zimmerman points out some things he's like to see more data on, things that few others mention. Gun safety training, he notes, for example, hasn't really been evaluated to determine if it is effective and whether safety training and programming should vary depending on the age of those trained, student experiences, and potential uses for the firearms.

He points to the need for successful technology solutions to allow or prevent the use of a firearm, and then the research that must follow. Above all, Zimmerman believes in creating safer schools begins with building a stronger violence prevention ecology in a community whether that be by cleaning up vacant properties, adding more green space, supporting community policing, creating more youth programming, keeping more community eyes on the streets, or helping kids to develop coping skills that stop them from resolving conflict with a gun.

> We're trying to work with them in schools and not criminalize a kid who acts out. Their brains aren't fully functioning. What we want to do is channel that energy in positive ways and support the kids. I'm an eternal optimist. I just believe we can do better, and we will do better if there's a will to do it. We have to get away from this, 'Oh, it's politics.' 'You're a Democrat,' or 'You're a Republican' and 'I own and gun so I'm a Republican.' There's a lot of Democrats who own guns and hunt and so it's not about politics or the Second Amendment. It's about what do we need to do to create a better place for all of us to live?
>
> At the end of the day, we all want to go to the city to see the

> museum, to go to dinner, or go to a ballgame. We want to be able to have our rural communities not be so economically depressed that people are killing themselves. We talked about how 90 percent of the suicide attempts with a gun are successful, yet 90 percent of the people who try to commit suicide, if they get help, do not try again. The finality of a firearm in a suicide context does not give anybody a second chance. They get the help they need, and they overcome it. How can that be bad for families and the fabric of the nation?
>
> I don't get it honestly. We've somehow vilified each other, and we have to start coming together to solve this problem, just like we did with cars.

With Marc's optimism, here is a look at promising might-happen ideas you may want to use in gun conversations.

Some of these ideas are already written into local laws in some states. Some are less controversial than others. If you don't know where to start in a conversation about guns, each is worth discussing calmly, no matter your position.

In the last chapter, I noted that local laws can be good incubators for ideas that might work on the national stage. Ongoing research will reveal more about the success of these many laws and policies such as one-gun-a-month purchase limits, waiting periods for cash to carry, red flag laws, and limitations on the purchase of ammunition and high-capacity magazines.

Additional localized solutions should be part of your discussions. Safety may be about limiting where guns can be carried, providing more security in some locations, and using gun detection systems in schools, businesses, and public places. It can also be about gun safety training for people of all ages, free distribution and encouraged use of trigger locks, and enhanced systems to take tips from the community about potential gun violence.

Learn more about these initiatives and support the one that you think might happen to help reduce gun violence.

Mandatory Reporting of Stolen Firearms and Ammunition

Federal law does not require individual gun owners to report the loss or theft of their firearm to police, but licensed dealers must. An estimated 380,000 guns are stolen annually, but only about 40 percent of these are reported to police. Multiple research efforts point to the prevalent use of stolen guns in crime.

Thirteen state laws have statutes that require some combination of reporting for lost or stolen guns, and each law is nuanced about the time needed to report, the risk to the gun owner for failing to report, and several other details. Reporting requirements can be written with incentives. In New Jersey, for example, the registered owner of an assault weapon is civilly liable for any damages resulting from a crime unless the owner reports the theft to law enforcement within 24 hours of their knowledge of the theft.

Though some people voluntarily report stolen firearms, a more complete database would help federal, state, and local law enforcement solve crimes.

Secure Storage for Guns in Homes

In 2022, the *New England Journal of Medicine* reported that firearms-related deaths were the leading cause of death among American children and adolescents aged one to 19, according to the CDC.

Unsecured guns in homes are to blame, sometimes ending up in a double tragedy when a child finds a gun and kills a sibling. Only a handful of states mandate secured storage in a home, and another dozen have specific laws that allow charges to be brought against adults when a child accesses a gun. The CDC reports that nearly two in 10 firearms injuries are unintentional.

Laws that mandate secure storage would help curb the reality that millions of kids live in a home with unsecured guns. Secured storage laws would likely prevent hundreds of thousands of guns stolen each year for use in other crimes.

Creative manufacturers have scores of ways to secure your firearms that still allow you to access them quickly in an emergency. Some are designed to look like furniture or other objects to deter thieves. Gun owners who don't know about these solutions simply aren't looking for them, and a law might encourage them to be more proactive.

The CDC has a dedicated web page just to encourage better safety practices for firearms injury prevention. Pro and anti-gun organizations alike advocate for safer storage of guns. The National Shooting Sports Foundation's Project ChildSafe, for example, emphasizes the importance of storing firearms unloaded and locked, with ammunition secured separately.

What are the customs in your home, the homes of your family and friends, and in your community? Does your neighborhood or school district host events to talk about gun safety? Maybe they should. Saving more children might happen if gun owners changed their habits, and if secure storage laws could be passed, nationally or locally. It's worth discussing.

More Extensive Suicide Prevention Efforts

According to the CDC, suicide is the leading cause of death in the US, and more than half of the 45,979 suicides in 2020 were firearms related.

Suicides using firearms are fatal 90 percent of the time, but suicides using any other means are fatal only four percent of the time, making firearms and suicide a devastating combination. How dangerous?

Though three times as many women attempt suicide, men are four times more likely to kill themselves, simply because 90 percent of them choose a gun to commit the act.

Our gun discussion can include how to develop and support programs for those in crisis.

One tentative positive: in 2022, a national dedicated phone number was established, 9-8-8, like the nationally recognized 9-1-1. The 988 Suicide and Crisis Lifeline is still relatively unknown, but it is gaining ground as a place to call or text if you are experiencing mental health-related distress or are worried about a loved one who may need crisis support. You can chat via 988lifeline.

I say it's tentative because not enough people know about this new effort and not enough funding is going into making 988 successful. I recently spoke to one police department official who admitted they didn't answer the 988 calls because they didn't have the manpower.

Share information about the new 988 effort and make sure your community has funds to support both answering and handing the call and it just might happen.

Red Flag Laws

Helping people in distress who also own guns is a challenge. Many states have tried to tackle this challenge head on using Extreme Risk Protection Orders (ERPOs), commonly referred to as red flag laws.

Since first appearing on the Connecticut legislative agenda after the Sandy Hook massacre, these laws allow a court to temporarily order the removal of guns from a person's home if a judge finds cause to believe the person is a danger to themselves or others. Though state laws vary, guns often must be returned in a fixed time after the decision, such as two weeks or six months.

The law can be useful when someone is identified as a potential threat to others, including in domestic disputes. A mandatory legal process is helpful in domestic violence cases where some witnesses might be reluctant. They are also used to remove firearms in the home of a person who has attempted or might attempt suicide.

Indiana documented a 7.5 percent reduction in firearm suicides in the 10 years following the enactment of its ERPO law. State laws vary, but most are like the New York's application for a Temporary ERPO that allows the petitioner to be a police officer, district attorney, family or household member, principal, or chief school officer, or any one of several licensed individuals in the medical world.

A handful of check boxes offer suggested concerns such as an instance where the person threatened violence to self or others, violated a protection order or previous ERPOs, recklessly displayed or used a firearm, has been convicted of an offense involving a weapon, recently acquired weapons and ammunition, or has a recent or ongoing abuse of controlled substances or alcohol.

The basic description belies the complex application that begins with a petition and requires a court hearing with a gun owner. In New York, a judge evaluates the petition and must believe the allegation that the person who has access to firearms is "likely to engage in conduct that would result in serious harm to self or others."

The time involved is an inherent risk when law enforcement seeks to get firearms out of the hands of a potentially dangerous person.

Opponents to ERPOs say anyone can locate a licensed firearms dealer who may be willing to temporarily store a gun for a fee, so the government doesn't need to get involved.

Virginia, the District of Columbia, and at least 19 other states now have a red flag law. The new Biden federal gun legislation is sending money to states to support the operating costs both in court and the clerk's office. Federal funds are also earmarked to help states initiate red flag laws.

A 1999 Duke University study of Connecticut's red flag law

estimated that for every 10 to 20 firearms surrendered, a life from a potential suicide was saved. An NPR-PBS NewsHour-Marist poll in 2022 found that 73 percent of Americans back red flag laws, including 60 percent of Republicans and 61 percent of gun owners. Local law enforcement in some communities, however, refuses to apply the law despite its documented successes. Opponents point to terrible shootings and say a red flag law would not have helped or was ineffective. This misses the point. Any instance where a red flag law prevents a death is a win, even if we can't count all of them.

"I don't have kids in my home, so I don't need to lock my guns up."

"Good gun safety is about getting into good habits, like always putting on a seat belt. I don't have kids at my house, but I lock my guns up. I know they are safely away if someone breaks into my home and they are safe from kids who might come by, snooping neighbors, or even the cleaning people. Better safe than sorry."

Enhanced Red Flag Laws

Potentially game-changing, enhanced red flag laws might happen if one or more states are willing to take this aspirational concept and run with it. It's an idea born from my many conversations with law enforcement and lawyers who express frustration about a loophole in red flag laws.

If you haven't heard this term, enhanced red flag laws, it's probably because I made it up.

Current red flag laws require a petition to be filed and a probable cause hearing, before firearms can be removed from the home of a person deemed to be a danger to themselves or others. This seems so contrary to what we have done in the past and I'm not sure how laws and policies have developed that favor leaving guns at volatile scenes.

Today, if a law enforcement officer is in a person's home and has probable cause to believe that person is a danger to himself of others, police can arrest that person. A prompt appearance in front of a judge would allow for the return of the guns if the confiscation was deemed in violation of the 4th Amendment, which is an unreasonable seizure.

Absent the visual brandishing of a weapon at another person, if that same law enforcement officer sees a weapon in that home during a dispute between two people, the officer can only take away firearms on the property if they know about them and the owner consents.

The implications in domestic violence cases are hopefully obvious, but those incidents are discussed in more detail later in this chapter so not belabored here. A person escalating in violence against an intimate partner and other family members, for example, may be on a pathway to violence. But without imminent danger, that person cannot be arrested, or the firearms removed.

The officer can, in many states, file a red flag petition asking a court to determine whether firearms should be removed for some period. Then the officer must return to the home and try to collect the firearms.

Red flag laws have inherent limitations. Filing paperwork takes time. Court hearings take time. And police must then return to the house to retrieve firearms from unwilling participants. If states require the person impacted to voluntarily turn in their guns to police, these orders can still be ignored, leaving police another task, to enforce the order.

Law enforcement impounds cars on the street to insure drivers won't climb back behind the wheel. They take away guns and knives from people they encounter on the street and when making arrests.

Legislators and policy makers should consider what we can do to better empower police who must act in the murky zone between the marriage of dangerous people and their access to guns.

Some Version of a SECURE Firearms Act

Introduced with identical language by Illinois Senator Richard J. Durbin in the Senate, and Illinois Representative Bradley Scott Schneider in the House, some version of the Safety Enhancements for Communities Using Reasonable and Effective (SECURE) Firearm Storage Act is directed solely at the action of firearms merchants.

The SECURE act would mandate that federal firearms licensee (FFLs) secure all firearms when their store is closed. FFLs would either need to fasten firearms to an anchored steel rod or store them in a locked safe or gun cabinet. Guns stolen from dealers are often used for criminal activity and sponsors of the bill note that a study of the time between 2012 and 2018 identified nearly 14,800 guns previously reported as lost or stolen from gun dealers recovered from crime scenes.

Support for this law might be easier to obtain if it had been introduced with less concern for a fancy mnemonic name and more concern to identifying it as supporting overnight safe storage of firearms at gun stores.

Proof of Insurance for Gun Owners

One city in California is taking an intriguing tack as it seeks to shift the financial burden of gun violence to gun owners. In 2022, the City of San Jose passed an ordinance requiring all gun owners to carry and provide proof of liability insurance coverage for accidental firearms-related death injury or property damage.

"While the Second Amendment protects the right to bear arms, it does not require taxpayers to subsidize gun ownership," Mayor Sam Liccardo said.

City residents have incurred an estimated $442 million in gun-related costs each year, he said. The insurance would be similar to the insurance required for owning a car or home. The accompanying $25 fee is slated to go towards community-based gun violence reduction programs. Failure to comply risks fines, fees, and the potential impounding of weapons subject to a due process hearing.

The anticipated legal challenges are underway, but attorneys representing the city are confident diligence in designing the ordinance will keep it on the books.

"Insurance is a way to offset the financial costs rather than leave it all in the hands of the victims," said Tamarah Prevost, a partner at Cotchelle, Pitre, and McCarthy LLP, representing the city for free. It's a good solution to the ever-exploding access to weapons, she said. Auto insurers use risk-adjusted premiums to reward good drivers and incentivize the use of airbags and other safety features, the city's ordinance notes. Firearms insurers could incentivize the taking of safety classes, use of gun safe, installation of trigger locks, and other risk reducing options.

The insurance industry will no doubt be watching the court results. They have paid out plenty in legal actions after a tragedy. In 2022, the gun manufacturer Remington agreed to pay $73 million to the families of nine Sandy Hook school shooting victims. To step around the federal law protecting gun manufacturers, the family had alleged the company's marketing of the weapon violated a Connecticut consumer law by purposefully marketing the AR-15-style rifle to troubled men like the killer.

Continued novel efforts like this might explain why some gun and ammunition manufacturers, too, have repositioned themselves and sold off manufacturing companies. They likely want to avoid the legal quagmire resulting from many shootings.

San Jose's effort is a model for communities willing to look for creative solutions.

Reporting for Certain Mental Health Matters

Mental health diagnoses and care are not, in and of themselves, indicative of firearms violence, according to the National Counsel for Mental Wellbeing, and truthfully, seemingly everyone who has done research in this area.

But federal law prohibits gun sales to people who have been adjudicated mentally defective, found not guilty by reason of insanity, or involuntarily committed to a mental health institution. Just about every person I speak with—both gun and non-gun owners—believe background checks could prevent someone with a serious mental health and historical mental health issues from buying and using a gun to commit a violent act.

The challenge is getting that information accurately into the systems used to do background checks on firearms sales, most notably the FBI's National Instant Criminal Background Check System, NICS.

Though many individuals have been involuntarily committed to mental health facilities or have had court orders adjudicating them a danger to themselves and others, reporting that information to the NICS system often does not occur. Some states completely refuse to report the adjudications and others are sporadic. Sometimes the refusal is because of a lack of funding to input the data, other times it is a lack of understanding about what to report. To overcome the budget challenges locally, a federal law passed in 2022 included funding to support this and other programs targeted at mental wellness and gun violence. Sometimes it's a political decision or just a lower priority for state and local officials.

The killers at Virginia Tech, the Navy Yard in Washington D.C., and the First Baptist Church in Sutherland Springs, Texas, met the criteria, but their situations were never reported to the NICS. This isn't a system to capture all people diagnosed with mental health conditions but rather those who have met certain criteria, such as involuntary commitments for mental health care.

We can make progress to improve reporting that could separate troubled people from firearms purchases, and it might happen if we can support the mandatory reporting and the funding to support the manpower to enter the proper information into NICS.

In 2018, Congress passed the Fix NICS Act to improve reporting requirement for the US Attorney General and federal agencies designed to improve reporting compliance requirements. The 2022 annual NICS report indicated has improved reporting by federal, state, tribal, and local agencies. This is a good example of a change most people have likely never heard about, that can have a big impact.

The newly passed NICS Denial Notification Act of 2022 may also improve NICS data collection since it requires FFLs to report a denial to law enforcement within 24 hours of the denial.

Increase the Number of Days to Perform a Background Check

Better data in NICS, spurred on by the Fix NICS Act, could not help the FBI's workload when extraordinary firearms sales prompted a record 39.6 million background check requests in 2020.

Most people may be unaware that when a NICS check cannot be completed in the three days allowed, and a gun transaction occurs, the NICS Section seeks to complete the background check, anyway. If the background is resolved and the FBI determines that the firearms purchaser is not allowed to own the gun, the FBI then issues a seizure order to the ATF. ATF agents then must seek to find the individual and seize the gun. In 2020, the FBI referred more than 6,300 seizure orders to the ATF. In 2021, they issued 5,200.

Though this is a very small number of potential sales, consider that the NICS Section annual reports already recognized between 400,000 and 500,000 background checks are unable to be completed within the three-day time period each year.

NRA officials are vocal about not extending the three-day period even though it would potentially impact just over one percent of all background checks performed. The result is guns in the hands of people who would not have been allowed to buy them, creating a public safety risk when crimes are committed with them, as has happened. ATF agents seeking to retrieve these guns are exposed to potential risk and agency resources are further stretched to meet the need. The ATF doesn't have the manpower to execute all the seizures every year more seizure orders are referred, compounding the problem. Extending the time period should cut back on untimely backgrounds check completions, keeping firearms out of the hands of thousands of those who are not legally allowed to carry them. In addition, the extension will reduce the time consuming and potentially dangerous effort to seize the gun by the ATF. The cost of trying is non-existent, so why not try it?

Background Checks for Those Under the Age of 21

How background checks are done has already been extensively discussed above, but one recent change in federal law is worth mentioning. A federal law passed in 2022 included a provision to enhance background checks for gun purchases between the ages of 18 and 21, mandating a check of local police records as well as state juvenile and mental health records. These backgrounds are referred to as U21 checks by the FBI's NICS team.

I checked in with the NICS team just as they were setting up the federal mechanisms to conduct the expanded background checks. With only a handful of states obligated to do the check in the first seven weeks, the team conducted 19,425 U21 checks. Time will tell if this helps reduce gun violence, but it might happen.

"I don't lock my gun up because I might need to get it in an emergency."

"Firearms deaths are the leading cause of death in the United States for children and adolescents, so do you warn friends and family? There are several options for locking up your guns that leave them readily accessible if you need to get to them quickly. If you are interested, I can show you gun safes that unlock using your fingerprint as well as other options."

Regulation Impacting the Availability of High Capacity Magazines, Rapid Fire Equipment, and Semi-Automatic Firearms

Discussion of these types of weapons and tools always raises the ire of everyone in the room. But many states are passing laws that will impact the purchases, ownership, and control of semiautomatic pistols and rifles, magazines, other firearms tools, and ammunition. Some laws, for example, limit the amount of ammunition that can be sold or limited capacity magazines. A federal law would be more efficient.

The reality is that some of the most heinous shootings that have ever occurred in America involved firearms with high-capacity magazines that allow rapid, continuous, firing with few magazine changes and fewer chances for those in the path to escape.

Stepping back and looking at the unvarnished and often ugly facts is key to fruitful negotiations. Only then can we continue these sometimes-uncomfortable conversations that need to include a discussion that stretches beyond our own personal desires to societal needs.

Though there are some practical uses for rifles, we should talk about who and when access should be given to a tool with three, four, or ten times more destructive power than some handguns. That includes acknowledging that 100-round magazines aren't designed for hunting animals.

Currently, most American adults can own these items, and many who do keep them more as trophies in locked or unlocked cases. It would be naïve to turn away from conversations about the potential benefits of looking at who can buy and carry around semiautomatic handguns, rifles, and high-capacity magazines.

Being safe and feeling safe are both important goals. Few gun owners believe someone should be able to strap an AR-15 style weapon around their shoulder and take a stroll into their local grocery store or voting booth. But it is done.

This important discussion might happen if we focus on both what not only will keep us safe, but also what will make us feel safe.

Supporting and Strengthening Domestic Violence Laws

Domestic abusers are incessant controllers, often using the threat of violence and physical force to dominate. Abusers with guns are the most minacious, using the gun to strike fear in all around them.

Why are aspects of domestic abuse on my might-happen list? Though there is little doubt about the connection between guns and domestic abusers, many loopholes in laws and policies keep guns in the hands of abusers. We need to do better.

In one research by DOJ, it estimated that 45 percent of all female homicide victims over a six-year period were killed by an intimate partner. And Everytown for Gun Safety reports that every month 70 women are shot and killed by an intimate partner and nearly one million women alive today have reported being shot or shot at by intimate partners.

If you don't know a woman who has been a victim of domestic

violence or has a friend who was, you probably haven't asked those around you. More than half of intimate partner homicides nationwide involve guns, according to Johns Hopkins Center for Gun Violence Solutions.

In 2009, researchers at Hopkins' Bloomberg School of Public Health analyzed US laws focused on guns and domestic violence. They found that intimate partner assaults involving a gun were three times more likely to result in homicide than those involving a knife, and 23 times more likely to result in death than those involving bodily force alone.

So why then aren't more universal efforts made to separate firearms from domestic abusers? It's a conversation worth having.

About 20 states have versions of laws that allow courts to require batterers to surrender firearms as a term of the protective order. But that same Hopkins research found the laws were not consistently enforced and sometimes judges failed to order firearms removed from the abuser's control. Some laws rely on the abuser to voluntarily turn in their guns, or the police to decide whether to remove guns.

As a prosecutor, I saw first-hand the pressure put on judges to cut defendants a break with requests to waive fines, jail time, and block forfeitures of guns. Abusers in their Sunday suits were common in my courthouse, apologizing for letting things get "a little out of hand."

When I was a prosecutor, Illinois passed a law requiring responding police on a domestic abuse call to take one person away from the home for an overnight cooling-off period in jail. This helped the police immensely because they could explain that they had no discretion, and it sometimes gave an abused person the opportunity to move to safety with the kids.

A variety of federal and state laws prohibit someone from buying a firearm if they are convicted of certain crimes that involve stalking, beating, or even killing a domestic partner. No federal and few state laws I am aware of require every person convicted of these crimes to voluntarily turn in their guns. To make that happen, state and local officials must take additional steps if a legal mechanism is available.

Eighteen states have laws addressing the seizure of firearms at the scene of domestic violence, according to the Battered Women's Justice Program. Only eight require police to seize weapons used or threatened to be used and another seven give police discretion to remove an involved weapon. Three of those states give law enforcement discretion to go beyond and take other firearms present. Many states limit the seizure to guns in plain view of the responding officers or only weapons discovered if the officer is allowed permission to search for weapons. Few state laws allow the seizure of ammunition.

Even if taken, ten of the 18 states require the return of the weapons in a time period as short as seven days unless the firearm is needed as evidence in a future court proceeding.

Often when a gun is removed from a home, it must be returned to its owner when the court matter is finished, unless other legal steps are taken. Guns taken from people are often turned over to someone of their choice, a parent, grandparent, or spouse. Those firearms often end up back in the hands of the abuser. That continues to leave firearms in the hands of even convicted domestic abusers unless someone steps in to change the situation. And relying on the person who is abused to do that is a non-starter.

Domestic abusers and stories of gun violence abound, such as guns raised to a woman's head, guns pointed at children to cause agony to a partner, and pistol whippings. Often, the last act in a long line of such abuses is murder.

We have come far in offering assistance. The National Domestic Violence Hotline can be reached by dialing 1.800.799.SAFE (7233). A live chat is available at https://www.thehotline.org, and live text can begin when you text "START" to 88788.

But changes in laws and policies drag behind, particularly in states where the laws do not aggressively protect the abused.

Research continues to strengthen our understanding of violence committed against intimate partners and violence against family members when it involves a larger plan to murder people. FBI research on active shooters found that often family and friends, former lovers, bosses, or co-workers are among the first victims. In the FBI's initial research on active shooter that I authored, about 10 percent of the active shooters targeted family members—with these often being the first to die. Another 10 percent targeted estranged or current wives or girlfriends.

Programs that separate abusers from their guns are solutions worth pursuing, but they require focus in each community.

Though disarming potential abusers has been shown effective in giving abusers a cooling-off period, surveys of law enforcement show officers are disinclined at times to seize guns, despite the danger to victims and children. According to the Battered Women's Justice Program, some police departments may not have the ability or desire to store weapons safely for a potential return. In addition, inadequate training for officers might make them uncertain about the extent of their authority and the benefits of removing the guns from that environment.

This isn't just a law enforcement matter. Many victims of domestic violence know their state laws on protective orders, firearms removal options, and how to best prevent their abuser from transferring firearms to someone who will simply return them. As friends, neighbors, and co-workers of those abused, we too can help by watching for and supporting the abused individuals hidden around us.

Aggressively working to pass stronger laws to protect the abused and fund enforcement will lead to a decrease in gun violence against intimate partners.

But I need to add a caveat. The US Supreme Court's 2022 decision in *New York Pistol* may have upended every bit of law in this area, perhaps unintentionally. Shortly after that decision, a 5th Circuit Court of Appeals decided the case of a Texas abuser and somewhat astonishingly concluded that to follow the US Supreme Court's decision might mean prohibiting the removal of guns from a domestic abuser.

Some background on the case.

The plaintiff in the case had been prohibited from carrying a gun after a protective order was entered as part of a resolution of abuse charge involving his girlfriend. But in February 2023, that Court ruled that the Second Amendment allows people under protective orders for committing domestic violence to keep their guns.

The Court entered this order even when evidence showed he had been involved in five shootings around Arlington, Texas. He shot at someone's house after selling them prescription narcotics. After getting into a car accident, he shot at a car, returned in another vehicle, and shot at the car again. Three days before Christmas, he shot at a constable's car. And after New Year's Day, he fired shots into the air outside a Whataburger after his friend's credit card was declined.

But in ruling in favor of the defendant, the majority opinion noted that "while hardly a model citizen, [the defendant] is nonetheless part of the political community entitled to the Second Amendment's guarantees, all other things equal."

This ruling is just one of many but speaks to the uncertainty that now exists on myriad domestic violence-related matters. The nearly endless cases that are now flowing toward federal district and appellate courts decisions will likely take years to provide clarity on when if ever intimate partners can be protected from gun-carrying domestic abusers.

Gun Safety Training

In a country filled with firearms, safety training should be more available for everyone. Though perhaps an unattainable goal, many believe no one should be able to own or touch a gun without comprehensive training in firearms safety and security. Many point out it is like getting a driver's license. Only a few states have these requirements.

Should everyone buying a gun be required to show they have taken a current gun safety class? Many other countries mandate this type of training. Some countries, like Switzerland, hold firearms competitions for teens, inherently requiring discipline and training in firearms safety.

Some states and school districts are considering offering gun safety classes like you would offer physical education classes in high school.

But gun safety training in schools is a complicated nut to crack. Some say that would encourage the purchase of more firearms. Some say it's training people to use guns. Some say they don't want their tax money spent that way. And money for gun safety may not be at the top of the list in districts where teacher salaries and programming are being cut.

Living in a country with more guns than people, it also seems to make sense to ensure everyone has some basic safety training available if they desire it. Firearms safety training must also focus on preservation of life.

THOUGHTS ABOUT MYTHS AND FACTS

As we talk about solutions to gun violence, don't make the mistake of attributing the violence to random causes that there is no research to support.

Most people are killed by someone they know, and more are killed at home than out in public, in school, or at work. And domestic terrorists are a significantly bigger threat to US citizens than foreign terrorists.

In my book *Stop the Killing: How to End the Mass Shooting Crisis*, I talk about some myths and mistaken beliefs worth noting. Playing video games, serving in the armed services, and receiving mental health care services are not predictive actions of those who commit violence.

Remember, as pointed out in chapter one, firearms homicides disproportionately impact Blacks, Hispanics, and other ethnic communities.

An endless amount of data shows this to be true. The point in putting this into my might-happen chapter is two-fold. Black Americans, aged 15 to 34, experience the highest rates of gun homicides across all demographics. American Indian and Native Alaskan women are killed by intimate partners at a rate four times higher than White women. And 60 percent of gun deaths among Hispanic and Latino people are gun homicides.

It's okay that you didn't know these facts, but continue to have an open mind and do some research that is well sourced in this area, so you are better equipped to have a conversation about the disparate impact of gun violence on various communities. It's important to not to just say "I didn't know" or "it doesn't happen to those around me." The bottom line is, it is important to advocate for funding and programs with an overlay that recognize some communities need more assistance than others.

This is an aspirational and incomplete list, but a good start. We are all on the same life raft together to sink or swim. And no one wants to live anymore in a world where we fear going to school, the library, work, or a movie. So, please consider what you can do in this monumental challenge.

"I can't talk about guns because everytime I try to do that it just starts an argument."

"How about if you try with me? I won't argue and I'll be a good listener. Talking about guns can be difficult. Some people just want to tell you their opinions without being open-minded. I find myself asking those people to explain their thoughts without interjecting my own opinions early in the discussion, and that helps create a conversation. If I say, 'What experiences do you have with guns?' I am more apt to understand where they are coming from."

Epilogue

In the 1930s, President Franklin D. Roosevelt (FDR) and his administration struggled to help 11 million people unemployed, and a country thrust into an unimaginable economic depression. Billions of dollars were dumped into often controversial programs. FDR employed a bit of spaghetti-thrown-at-the-wall methodology when urgency was everything.

Every middle school student learns about the Works Progress Administration, a program that lasted eight years and cost taxpayers an estimated $11 billion, $200 billion in today's dollars. Those hired built airports, bridges, roads, and parks, most still in use today. Also, among the 3.5 million people hired were artists and painters who created the now iconic images of Americans in various walks of life on the walls of public buildings.

I fear my analysis of solutions to gun violence is impacted by my life's experiences with limited authority. As a lawyer, I tried to work within existing laws and court decisions. As an FBI agent, I often told people I viewed the FBI as the civilian Marines; we do the job with tools we have.

I cower at the uphill climb to find billions to increase or build new federal infrastructures, whether it is to buy back, register or trace guns, re-tool US businesses, or re-invent the infrastructure necessary to support sweeping changes in law, regulations, and policies.

America has faced bigger challenges head on, pouring money into solutions, changing laws, and altering our way of life—for the better. Social Security, Medicare, and Medicaid reflect our country's desire to ensure the older and challenged populations aren't left to die on the street or in their homes. As a nation, we saw the good in creating a social safety net. Retooling of these programs is always underway, but in the meantime, the programs exist and help millions of people every day obtain needed medical care, feed themselves, and pay their rent.

In 2008, the federal government extended support to what would total over $81 billion, that's $116 billion in today's dollars, to aid the US auto industry—then in peril of collapse. The decision by President George W. Bush's administration, and supported throughout President Barack Obama's administration, cost US taxpayers $10.2 billion alone. That key American industry, and the people employed by it, continues today, not only in my hometown of Detroit but across the country and around the world.

In America, we continue to solve larger-than-life problems, and we are damn good at it.

In 2020, when the COVID pandemic hit, eventually killing more than one million US citizens, two White House administrations worked to bring things under control by providing the financial infrastructure needed to tame this public health crisis.

When COVID added to an already stressed farming industry struggling with the cost of tariff wars, for example, direct farm aid to them climbed from $11.5 billion in aid in 2017 to more than $32 billion in 2020, discussed in a Politico story by Ryan McCrimmon in April 2020.

In 2021, the $2.2 trillion price tag of the Coronavirus Aid, Relief and Economic Security Act included public-health-focused aid that provided paid sick leave, relief to small businesses, and tax breaks to hospitals and health care programs. The $1.9 trillion American Rescue Plan Act that followed focused on supporting businesses and provided unemployment assistance to those impacted by the pandemic. It included $54 billion just for the US airline industry, as well as billions more for emergency grants and loans for small businesses.

When $50 billion in COVID money went to the Federal Emergency Management Agency for vaccine distribution and assistance, those supporting the money for FEMA viewed it as part of the comprehensive battle plan to an overwhelming public health challenge.

Firearms casualties are an acknowledged and undeniable public health crisis.

Sometimes we think we are arguing about whether we need new laws or policies, when in fact we are disagreeing about the resulting impact. Once implemented, time and research will tell us if we are going in the right direction.

We don't always know what will work when we make an investment, but our lives and the lives of those we love and care about make it worth trying.

Perhaps we need to be a bit more like FDR in our efforts. Only then might we live in a gun culture we say we want, not in the gun culture we have accepted and embraced.

Conversation Starters

I know we disagree about whether people should be able to own guns, but can we agree to disagree about that and then talk about how we might better tackle some solutions to gun access for those who are in a mental health crisis? To work towards solving gun violence, we have to be able to talk about it.

I know we disagree about the right to carry guns concealed or in public, but can we agree to disagree about that and then talk about ideas to keep people safe in public spaces?

I know we disagree about many aspects of the Second Amendment, but can we agree to disagree about that and talk about some ideas to end gun violence with our existing laws?

I know we disagree about many aspects in the gun debate, but can we agree to disagree about that and talk about some ways to better combat suicide in our community?

I know we disagree about whether people should be able to own guns, but can we agree to disagree about that and then talk about practical solutions to teach gun safety to those around them? We all want safer communities.

I know we disagree about whether all semi-automatic rifles and handguns should be confiscated, but can we agree to disagree about that and then talk about teachers and others being able to carry a gun in school? We all want to solve gun violence and the more we talk about this complicated problem, the closer we get to solutions.

I know we disagree about what guns people should be able to own, but can we agree to disagree about that and then talk about our mutual fear of shootings in schools or in the public, and some of the ways we might take away that fear, for our kids too, if we are better informed and prepared?

Conversations Inside

"Guns don't kill people, people kill people."

"I agree with that. The problem that I see is that troubled people with guns kill innocent people. Do you have practical ways to keep guns out of the hands of those troubled people? Most stop talking at this point or say it's all a mental health problem. But what about suicides, domestic violence, and accidental deaths?"

"Why on earth would you own a gun or keep one in your house?"

"I use mine for target practice, a sport I like. But I saw stats that said most people keep them for protection, so when I talk to people who have guns, I also try to remember they want that protection for themselves and their families."

"With all of these guns around, I am afraid to let my kids go to their friend's house. I'm afraid a gun is tucked in a drawer or on a shelf and my kid will pick it up."

"That's scary. I'm sure you're not alone. Before I allow my own kids to go inside another child's house, I insist on a visit so I can meet the parents face-to-face. I straight out ask if there are any guns in the house because I think people should be frank about that. Would you be comfortable doing that? You can also make your house the house where kids come over."

"I read that guns don't make homes safer; I don't believe that."

"Many studies validate this, even though people buy them for protection. An overwhelming number of guns are stolen from homes or are used in domestic violence situations. The overwhelming reason most suicides happen at home where people have access to guns and millions of guns are unsecured. Every year this also results in a few hundred unintentional shootings by kids who find them."

"I don't have kids in my home, so I don't need to lock my guns up."

"Good gun safety is about getting into good habits, like always putting on a seat belt. I don't have kids at my house, but I lock my guns up. I know they are safely away if someone breaks into my home and they are safe from kids who might come by, snooping neighbors, or even the cleaning people. Better safe than sorry."

"I don't lock my gun up because I need to be able to get to it fast."

"I get that. Actually, though, that's pretty dangerous because kids are pretty crafty and have been known to find them even if you think they are hidden. I can't imagine how I would feel if a kid found my gun and accidentally killed himself or someone else. In my home, we keep the guns locked up and teach gun safety. If you want, I could show you how quickly I can access the gun safe I own. There are gun safes that have quick access and can be hidden around the home too."

"I don't lock my gun up because I might need to get it in an emergency."

"Firearms deaths are the leading cause of death in the United States for children and adolescents, so do you warn friends and family? There are several options for locking up your guns that leave them readily accessible if you need to get to them quickly. If you are interested, I can show you gun safes that unlock using your fingerprint as well as other options."

"I don't know anything about guns, and I don't want my kids knowing about guns."

"I appreciate that guns are a scary topic, but the reality is that there are lots of guns in this country. I taught my kids about guns just to make sure they were safe if they ended up around one. I'd be happy to talk with you and your kids about gun safety, or even take you to the range to show you how to handle a gun safely, just in case."

"My sister wants to buy a gun for protection, but I told her she's nuts."

"Some people think a gun is a great equalizer in a confrontation, and I try to respect that, but it isn't always that simple. Studies show homes with guns have higher incidents of firearms deaths."

"I think it will be more dangerous and won't keep her safe."

"Have you thought about asking her how she thinks it will make her safer? You have a right to be concerned because carrying a gun is an enormous responsibility. You might ask her how she'll keep it secure, how much practice she'll have, and where she will carry it. I know that carrying a gun can often be cumbersome and not allowed in areas like parks, schools, and buildings, prompting people to leave their guns under car seats and in bags where they can be stolen. That's where most guns are stolen from."

"She's going to get it no matter what I say."

"You might take the time to talk to her about it more and maybe you will feel better, no matter what she decides. Make sure you discuss with her whether you would allow the gun at a family gathering or in your home too, if that might be an issue."

"That experiment by the Founding Fathers didn't work, so we need to repeal it."

"Many other countries allow citizens to own guns without having a Second Amendment, so I'm not sure that this is the quick solution to gun violence you are looking for. This is a democracy and right now the Constitution and the laws allow for gun ownership. Let's come up with something more immediate. I believe individual freedom to make our own choices is a very important concept for most Americans. I'd rather concentrate on insuring guns are safely handled and stored, and don't get into the hands of criminals or those who want to commit suicide."

"I think we should repeal the Second Amendment."

"That's cool. I'm not in that camp, but I respect you are. I believe the Second Amendment is there to protect citizens from abuse by the government and from other threats to our physical safety. No one is forced to own a gun. At the same time, no one should be prevented from owning a gun unless there is a good reason, so maybe we need to work better on those reasons."

"I'm afraid to talk to my kid about guns. It scares me."

"It might help if you focused on discussing something besides gun violence. I grew up in a house with several guns. They were locked up in my parents' bedroom and we knew we were not allowed to go in there. Mostly, those guns were used for small game and deer hunting. When those seasons came around every fall, my dad would bring out a gun and do some target shooting to get ready to go hunting. I learned to think of the guns as tools that were used for a specific purpose."

"The Second Amendment was written to protect citizens against a tyrannical federal government. Don't you believe in the Constitution? I should be able to carry any gun I want without a permit."

"I believe that's not a realistic fear, but my concern is that carrying a gun in public concealed is dangerous. I hear news stories about tempers flaring and shootings happening at bars, in stores, and in parks. When a gun is pulled to resolve an argument in public, that puts so many more people in danger."

"I think we shouldn't allow concealed carry."

"I respect that, it's just that that's the law right now here, and each community is setting its own standards, so you can work to change the law if you feel that strongly about it. Have you spoken to your congress people and local representatives?"

"I can't talk about guns because everytime I try to do that it just starts an argument."

"How about if you try with me? I won't argue and I'll be a good listener. Talking about guns can be difficult. Some people just want to tell you their opinions without being open-minded. I find myself asking those people to explain their thoughts without interjecting my own opinions early in the discussion, and that helps create a conversation. If I say, 'What experiences do you have with guns?' I am more apt to understand where they are coming from."

"I don't think there is any gun law or regulation that would work."

"I see it a little differently. We do have several laws and regulations on the books already. I see more of a challenge with enforcement. Most citizens are law-abiding and better enforcement would tell us which laws are working, and which ones might need to be changed. Have you seen anything on better funding for ATF and police enforcement?"

"Give me one good reason why anyone should be able to own a rifle?"

"That's a fair question. For me, there are two main reasons that I and many of my friends own rifles. The first is hunting. People hunt wild hogs, deer, bear, and wolves with rifles primarily because they can hit a target that is further away. There are millions of hunters in this country who enjoy this activity and handguns are difficult to use for this kind of hunting. I also know simple target shooting is very popular with rifles."

"My ten-year-old told me he heard a noise at school and he thought it was gunshots and was scared. I didn't know what to say to him. We just need to get rid of all the guns."

"I would have been scared too, and scared for my child. Did you tell him it was good he came to you with his fear? Also, I'd consider a call or visit to the school principal as a good place to start to try to figure out what really happened. Maybe don't jump right to any conclusions."

"Passing gun laws is the beginning of the slippery slope towards taking all our guns away, don't you think?"

"We have millions of guns in this country, so that's not really a realistic fear, but I appreciate that you might be tired of hearing it and you just don't want anyone messing with your guns. It is frustrating that gun violence involves a small number of people, but changes in laws impact law-abiding gun owners. If not gun regulations, do you have some concrete changes that might help?"

"I don't want my kid to have to do drills in school for a potential shooting, it's just scary and wrong."

"It is scary, but if we approach it as another aspect of safety drills, like fire and tornado drills, then they just view it as safety training for something that is not likely to happen. Truthfully, I think kids get this better than their parents do."

"I like the way the UK has laws that require people to get a license to carry a gun. That includes doing a background check that is more extensive than in the United States. You have to be interviewed and others must vouch for you."

"I don't want to get a license and have a background done. That invades my privacy."

"I appreciate your concern, but we get licenses to drive a car or pilot a plane. The background interviews in Europe are designed to identify people who may have mental wellness issues, temper issues, or other problems. It's worth giving up a bit of freedom to find those people who maybe shouldn't be allowed to own guns. What do you think?"

"I like Texas' new law eliminating licensing and training so now I can carry my handgun anywhere I want."

"I think that is sending us backwards. That's like allowing people to drive without any training, except this is allowing someone to carry a lethal weapon around in public. I don't think that makes us safer, do you?"

"The Supreme Court upheld the Second Amendment last year, so I don't think there is any point in talking about regulating guns."

"If you mean the New York case, the Bruen decision, I think you are misunderstanding the role of the Supreme Court. Just like the Court's decision in Heller in 2008, the justices were asked very narrow questions to evaluate whether a given state law was Constitutional. In both cases, the written opinions are very interesting reads about when and how firearms should be controlled. The Bruen case, for example, only dealt with a law on an individual's right to carry a handgun outside their home."

About the Author

Katherine Schweit is an attorney and retired FBI special agent who created and led the FBI's active shooter program after the horrible tragedy at Sandy Hook Elementary School.

She joined a White House team working on violence prevention matters led by then Vice President Biden. She authored the FBI's seminal research on active shootings, *A Study of 160 Active Shooter Incidents in the United States Between 2000 and 2013,* and was part of the crisis team responding to shooting incidents at the Holocaust Memorial Museum, the Pentagon, and the Navy Yard in the Washington, DC, area.

She is an executive producer on the award-winning film, *The Coming Storm*, widely used in security and law enforcement training throughout the United States and the State Department worldwide. This work earned her a second US Attorney General's outstanding contributions award.

Before starting her own consulting firm, Schweit Consulting LLC, she was the director for security training at a Fortune 300 company. A one-time print journalist and former assistant state's attorney in Chicago, she has published extensively, including opinion pieces in the *New York Times* and Chicago's *Daily Herald.* She is a recognized expert in active-shooter matters, crisis response, workplace violence, and corporate security policies and often is asked to provide on-air television commentary when tragedies occur.

She is a founding partner of the Bureau Consortium, a coordinated effort to join the best federal and local crisis experts with those who need them most. She regularly speaks to professional, government, and private organizations. She is a member of the Association of Threat Assessment Professionals, the International Association of Chiefs of Police, and the International Association for Healthcare Security and Safety, and is a certified compliance and ethics professional.

She is adjunct faculty at DePaul University College of Law and Webster University. She lives in Northern Virginia, outside of Washington, DC.

Made in the USA
Middletown, DE
23 May 2023